A Terrible Beauty

A Terrible Beauty

The Easter Rebellion and Yeats's "Great Tapestry"

Carmel Jordan

Lewisburg
Bucknell University Press
London and Toronto: Associated University Presses

Associated University Presses
440 Forsgate Drive
Cranbury, NJ 08512

Associated University Presses
25 Sicilian Avenue
London WC1A 2QH, England

Associated University Presses
2133 Royal Windsor Drive
Unit 1
Mississauga, Ontario
Canada L5J 1K5

The paper used in this publication meets the requirements
of the American National Standard for Permanence of Paper
for Printed Library Materials Z39.48-1984.

Library of Congress Cataloging-in-Publication Data

Jordan, Carmel, 1942–
    A terrible beauty.

    Bibliography: p.
    Includes index.
    1. Yeats, W. B. (William Butler), 1865–1939—
Political and social views. 2. Yeats, W. B. (William
Butler), 1865–1939—Knowledge—Ireland. 3. Ireland—
History—Sinn Fein Rebellion, 1916—Literature and the
rebellion. 4. Ireland in literature. I. Title.
PR5908.P6J67   1987   821'.8   86-47550
ISBN 0-8387-5107-5 (alk. paper)

Printed in the United States of America

For My Mother

Contents

Acknowledgments

Many individuals helped to make this book a reality. I am especially indebted to Professor Philip Sicker of Fordham University, whose insights into Yeats's nationalism proved invaluable. Professor Gale Schricker and Professor Joseph Grennen gave generously of their time and advice, and a Dissertation Fellowship from Fordham University made possible six months of research in Dublin. Professor Brendan Kennelly of Trinity College, Dublin, went out of his way to facilitate my research at the library there and gave me some excellent advice on Yeats. I would also like to thank Professor Martin Stevens of Baruch College for his constant encouragement and guidance.

A book begins as an idea, and an idea begins as a moment of curiosity. For such curiosity I am indebted to my family. I am especially grateful to my father, Edward Jordan, for reciting Yeats's poems to me as a child and for the many passionate discussions on Irish literature that we engaged in until his death. Thanks are also due to my two brothers, Edward and Robert Jordan, whose encyclopedic knowlege of Irish history and politics invoked in me, at an early age, a great curiosity about Irish nationalism. Finally, the debt I owe to my mother, Hilda Jordan, can never be fully acknowledged. My mother's idealism and sense of beauty has been an enduring influence throughout my life. Her financial and moral support during graduate school made possible the completion of *A Terrible Beauty*.

I owe a special debt to Eithne Bree, to Dr. Ann Ward, and to Ossama Sedky for their encouragement during the dark hours that sometimes accompany ambitious literary endeavors. I am especially grateful to Gretta Cachat who listened patiently to my ideas on Yeats, and to Rod Inger who fired my imagination with his provocative questions. Finally, I would like to thank Professor Victor Reed of Lehman College, in whose class my love of Yeats blossomed and who told me a long time ago that I would one day write a book on Yeats.

I wish to thank the following for permission to quote from published works:

Macmillan Publishing Co., Inc., A. P. Watt Ltd., on behalf of Michael B. Yeats and Macmillan London Ltd., for permission to quote from *The Poems of*

A Terrible Beauty

Introduction

REFERRING to the Druid-Christian matrix out of which Irish literature has evolved, Yeats, in "A General Introduction for my Work," writes: "Behind all Irish history hangs a great tapestry, even Christianity had to accept it and be itself pictured there. Nobody looking at its dim folds can say where Christianity begins and Druidism ends."[1] These words, written less than two years before his death, reflect Yeats's lifelong fascination with Ireland's Druid-Christian past and his belief that every aspect of Irish life has been influenced by that fertile synthesis. The "great tapestry" is central to Yeats's romantic nationalism and plays a key role in his perception of the Easter Rebellion as an episode in an ongoing "legend" of "terrible beauty." Just as the endlessly interlinking spiral patterns in the *Book of Kells* cannot be separated from each other without breaking the potency of their form, so too Yeats's poetry on the Rising cannot be fully appreciated without understanding the "tapestry" of allusion that lies behind it. Read against the background of that tapestry, Yeats's political poems and plays flower in all their symbolic richness.

The "Rose," "Cuchulain," the "fierce horsemen," and many other symbols of "terrible beauty" that pervade the landscape of Yeats's poems on the Rising find their roots in the great tapestry. In "Easter 1916," for example, the symbol of the stone, around which the poem revolves, has mythological, nationalistic and poetic associations that can be traced back to the dawn of Irish history. These associations give it a depth and resonance far beyond the immediate metaphorical implications discussed by critics.[2]

Most importantly, Yeats's concept of the Mask, which played such an important part in his perception of the Rising as drama, also finds its roots in Irish legend.[3] Yeats himself, in his autobiography, tells us that his first thoughts of the Mask came about as a result of stories he and Lady Gregory had heard about "changelings." According to Irish fairylore, the Sidhe sometimes kidnap a human individual and leave a Masklike image (a changeling) in his place. This ancient belief, Yeats tells us, inspired his "Doctrine of the Mask": "After many years that thought, others often found as strangely being added to it, became the thought of the Mask which I have used in these memoirs to explain men's characters."[4]

Thus, the symbols and Masks that are utilized by Yeats in his poems and plays on the Rising can be found in the archetypal images of Ireland's Druid-

Christian past. The 1916 poets, like Yeats, turned to that past for their inspiration. They invoked as the symbol of their movement the ancient warrior god Cuchulain: "When Pearse summoned Cuchulain to his side / What stalked through the Post Office?"[5] In 1916 the heroic Mask of Cuchulain served as a vehicle through which both the individual and the nation could be transformed. The leaders of the Rebellion belonged to a cult of Cuchulain and Yeats himself refers to Cuchulain, both in his letters and his literary works, as a symbol of the Rising.[6] Cuchulain epitomized not only the "terrible beauty" of the Rebellion, but the "terrible beauty" of Ireland herself and her long troubled history.

Critics have treated Cuchulain as a symbol of heroic courage and tragic joy.[7] The *Tain Bo Cuailnge*, the central saga of the tapestry, reveals, however, that Cuchulain was also a poet and that he was intimately tied to the sacrificial, mythological, and poetic traditions of Ireland that inspired the Rising. Cuchulain, like Pearse and his fellow poets, was a great lover of Mask and Image. During his courtship of Emer, for example, Cuchulain deliberately "masks" his words in the poet speech of ancient Ireland known as riddles."[8] When Laeg, his charioteer, appears dumbfounded by Cuchulain's symbolic conversation with Emer, Cuchulain tells him that he deliberately "put a cloak"[9] on his words so that the young girls nearby would not be able to understand the erotic content of their conversation.

As we step out of the pages of Irish mythology and into Irish history, we find that the tradition of using a poetic Mask spans the centuries. From her earliest origins, Ireland herself has been portrayed through a poetic Mask as a woman, but during the centuries of British occupation this literary device became a powerful political tool. Rather than risk accusations of treason, Irish poets "masked" their references to Ireland in metaphor and symbol, or, as Cuchulain would have it, they "put a cloak" on their words. In the Penal age, Aodh de Blacam observes, "the personification of Eire as the dis-crowned, wandering heart of beauty, became the most familiar symbol in the racial imagination."[10] "The Black Rose," "Inisfail," "Gile na Gile," and other poetic names for Ireland are all facets of Ireland's feminine Mask fashioned by her poet-lovers through the centuries. Yeats, the 1916 poets, and Bobby Sands continued to utilize the feminine Mask tradition in their poetry.

The concept of Mask, then, has been an inextricable part of the poetic landscape of Ireland from earliest times. An examination of Irish art and archeology, moreover, reveals that the fascination with Mask that we see in Yeats, in Wilde, and in the 1916 poets is rooted deep in the Celtic past. Ann Ross, in her study of the pagan Celts, writes that "stylized human Masks"[11] were a prominent motif in Celtic art. She notes that a fascination with such Masks continued in Ireland "to an almost bewildering degree"[12] right through the Middle Ages. The mysterious stone Masks that stare down at us from the arches of medieval Irish cathedrals testify to this fascination. They are ancient reminders of the barbaric splendor of Ireland's pagan past, and their sinister beauty recalls Yeats's reverence for the Mask: "A Mask will enable me to substitute for the face of some commonplace player, the fine invention of the sculptor. . . ."[13]

The fascination with Mask and Image that pervades Irish history reached its culmination in the Easter Rising. F. X. Martin, in "Myth, Fact, and Mystery," writes that the Rebellion was "staged consciously as a drama by its principal actors,"[14] and Yeats, in "Three Songs to the One Burden," refers to the background of the Rebellion as a "painted scene" and the participants in the Rebellion as actors: "Who was the first man shot that day? / The player Connolly."[15] Less than a year after the principal "players" in the Rising had been executed, the Irish writer P. Browne praises the ancient traditions and ideals that lay behind the Rebellion and motivated men like Pearse. He writes of Pearse that the ancient, medieval, and modern Gaelic currents met in him and that by his life and death he had become one with "Cuchulain, and Fionn and Oisin, with the early teachers, terrible or gentle, of Christianity . . . with Wolfe Tone and the United Irishmen, with Rossa, O'Leary, and the Fenians."[16] Browne observes that in Pearse "all the tendencies of Irish thought, culture, and nationality were more fully developed. He remains a symbol of the unbroken continuity and permanence of the Gaelic tradition . . . a second Cuchulain, who battled with a divine frenzy to stem the waves of the invading tide."[17]

This study carefully examines the "unbroken continuity and permanence of the Gaelic tradition" as it relates to Yeats and the Masks and Images of the Easter Rebellion. Chapter 1 discusses the distinct quality of the Irish imagination that created heroes like Cuchulain who sum up the imaginative history of Ireland in all its terrible beauty. The chapter stresses the imaginative link between ancient and modern Irish history and demonstrates how motifs and attitudes so evident in the Rising can be traced back ultimately to the great tapestry. Chapter 2 discusses Yeats's "Doctrine of the Mask" as it pertains to his poetry on the Rebellion and examines the fascination with Mask exhibited by the 1916 poets themselves. The chapter shows the reciprocal influence of Yeats and the 1916 poets upon each other and reveals how the poetic quality of the Rebellion confirmed Yeats's complex theories of the Mask. The last chapter discusses the imaginative unity of Yeats's Cuchulain plays and their connection with Yeats's poem, "Easter 1916." The chapter considers how Cuchulain's quest for beauty in these plays symbolically parallels the quest for beauty which lay at the back of the Rising and shows how the Masks of the various women of the Sidhe seen throughout the play cycle dissolve ultimately into one great Mask—a Mask that represents the fatal beauty of Ireland herself. The study demonstrates, finally, that any analysis of Yeats's poetry on the Rising which does not take into account the intricate mythological, historical, and poetic traditions of the great tapestry upon which this poetry draws will fail, ultimately, to do justice to the rich symbolic levels of meaning that characterize Yeats's political verse.

1
The Gaelic Tradition

I am Ireland:
I am older than the Old Woman of Beare.

Great my glory:
I that bore Cuchulain the valiant.

Great my shame:
My own children that sold their mother.

I am Ireland:
I am lonelier than the Old Woman of Beare.[1]

Padraic Pearse,
executed Kilmainham Jail
Dublin
3 May 1916

i

ON Easter Monday 1916, a handful of men took over the General Post Office in Dublin, raised the Irish flag from the window, and made a stand unparalleled in military history. For six days, these men, poorly clad and armed with little more than their dreams, held the British army at bay and proclaimed the birth of the Irish Republic. Although the insurrection was brutally crushed by the British and its leaders executed, it was a spiritual victory for the men involved, for they had awakened once again the soul of Ireland and paved the way for Irish freedom. They had created by their heroic defiance of the British on Easter Monday the "terrible beauty" of which Yeats writes in "Easter 1916":

> I write it out in a verse
> MacDonagh and MacBride
> And Connolly and Pearse
> Now and in time to be,
> Wherever green is worn,
> Are changed, changed utterly:
> A terrible beauty is born.[2]

The "terrible beauty" of the Easter Rebellion, which dramatically trans-formed the moral landscape of Ireland and dragged her away from "the formless spawning fury" of the "filthy modern tide" ("The Statues," 29) to an Ireland of fantastic horsemen and aristocratic warriors, is connected in Yeats's poetry with an ancient cultural emblem—the Mask of Cuchulain. In a letter to Edith Shackleton Heald written the year before his death, Yeats, referring to his poem "The Statues," writes: "Cuchulain is in the last stanza because Pearse and some of his followers had a cult of him. The Government has put a statue of Cuchulain in the rebuilt post office to commemorate this."[3] The tragic beauty of the Easter Rising and its inextricable connection with Cuchulain was still on Yeats's mind just before his death. He writes of it in his last play, *The Death of Cuchulain:*

> What stood in the Post Office
> With Pearse and Connolly?
> What comes out of the mountain
> Where men first shed their blood?
> Who thought Cuchulain till it seemed
> He stood where they stood?[4]

Why did the Mask of Cuchulain act as such a hypnotic symbol for both Yeats and the men of 1916? And how is the Mask of Cuchulain the perfect embodiment of that "terrible beauty" of "Easter 1916"? Yeats's theory of the heroic Mask offers some illumination:

> My mind began drifting towards that doctrine of "the Mask" which has convinced me that every passionate man . . . is, as it were, linked with another age, historical or imaginary, where alone he finds images that rouse his energy. Napoleon was never of his own time . . . but had some Roman emperor's image in his head and some condottiere's blood in his heart.[5]

The leaders of the Rebellion were certainly "linked with another age" when they took up their rifles against the British on Easter Monday, and that age was the heroic age of Cuchulain. Their imaginations rested not with the shopkeepers of modern Dublin who "But fumble in a greasy till / And add the halfpence to the pence" ("September 1913," 2–3), but with the Druids and warriors of ancient Ireland. They passionately embraced the Mask of Cuchulain and by so doing embraced both its terror and its beauty.

Cuchulain was the chief warrior of the Red Branch Cycle of Irish heroic tales, of which the *Tain Bo Cuailnge* (Cattle Raid of Cooley) is the mainstay. The *Tain*, which is the oldest vernacular epic in Western literature, is contained in several medieval manuscripts: the *Book of Leinster* (twelfth century), the *Book of the Dun Cow* (twelfth century), and the *Yellow Book of Lecan* (fourteenth century). The origins of the epic, however, are much older than these manuscripts. The language of the earliest form of the story goes back to the eighth century, and Irish scholars believe that many of the verse passages may be two centuries older.[6] It refers to events which took place before the coming of Christianity to Ireland, and, as a portrayal of Irish pagan civilization, the *Tain* and its ancillary stories are of the highest significance. In these stories Cuchulain represents all that is heroic, passionate, solitary, and tragic. Divinity and humanity meet in him, and he possesses the "terrible beauty" of one who is neither fully human nor fully divine but walks periously along the edge of both worlds. He is blessed by the gods with a volcanic energy that annihilates everything that opposes it. This energy is often sexually directed, and, in Yeats's play, *The Only Jealousy of Emer*, the singer describes Cuchulain as "that amorous violent man."[7] We shall see later that throughout the entire Cuchulain play cycle, sex and death are fatally linked.

What is particularly fascinating about Cuchulain as he is depicted in the ancient sagas, and what makes him such a fitting emblem for a rebellion that relied so much on the evocative power of Mask and Image, is that he is a great lover of Mask and Image himself. This important fact has been overlooked by critics in their discussion of Yeats's use of Cuchulain as a symbol in his poetry and plays. Critics assume that Yeats is using Cuchulain merely to reflect the typical attributes of the hero. They have treated Cuchulain as a symbol of heroic courage and tragic joy and a convenient symbol that Yeats appropriated for his own personal use.[8] As a result, Cuchulain's role in the Irish sagas as a poet who delighted in the intricacies of language as well as the intricacies of battle has been overlooked. And it is precisely this "poetic" aspect of his personality that makes him the ideal emblem for a rebellion "staged" by poets. A reading of *Cuchulain of Muirthemne*, for example, clearly reveals not only that Cuchulain had mastered the art of writing poetry, but that he considered that mastery as an essential part of his virility. When Emer asks Cuchulain for proof of his manhood, he boasts that as a young boy he was tutored by the Druid Amergin—the first poet of Ireland: "I stood by the knee of Amergin the poet, he was my tutor, so that I can stand up to any man, I can make praises for the doings of a king."[9] Cuchulain delights in using symbolic language. This is particularly evident when he comes to court Emer, for he deliberately disguises his words in the cryptic language of the Druid poets known as "riddles": "And he answered her in riddles, that her companions might not understand him. . . . While they were talking like this, Cuchulain saw the breasts of the maiden over the bosom of her dress, and he said: 'Fair is this plain, the plain of the noble yoke.'"[10] Emer answers in equally rich occult language, and the two engage in a lengthy, highly erotic conversation which becomes so symbolic, so filled with mythological references to legendary battles and gods that Cuchulain's charioteer, Laeg, is bewildered. Cuchulain later deciphers this symbolic language for Laeg, telling him that he deliberately "masked" his words so that the young girls with Emer would not understand their conversation:

When he was driving across the plain of Bregia, Laeg, his chariot-driver, asked him, "What, now, was the meaning of the words you and the maiden Emer were speaking together?" "Do you not know," said Cuchulain, "that I came to court Emer? And it is for this reason we put a cloak on our words, that the young girls with her might not understand what I had come for."[11]

Yeats, in his poem "Meeting," uses the word "cloak" in exactly the same way as Cuchulain:

> Hidden by old age awhile
> in masker's cloak and hood,
> Each hating what the other loved,
> Face to face we stood:
> "That I have met with such," said he
> "Bodes me little good."[12]

"Cloak" in the above lines is used as a synonym for "Mask"—"masker's cloak." In the Irish tradition, poets reaching across the space of a thousand years use the same images.

Yeats loved the "symbolic" quality of the conversation between Cuchulain and Emer and describes it as an excellent example of the "poet speech" of ancient Ireland, which requires for writing and understanding a "great traditional culture."[13] He praises the conversation for its heaping up of one mythological image upon another: "The mythological events Cuchulain speaks of give mystery to the scenery of the tales, and when they are connected with the Battle of Magh Tuireadh, the most tremendous of mythological battles, or anything else we know about, they are full of poetic meaning or historical interest."[14] It is fascinating that in 1902 Yeats, a modern Irish poet looking back through the mists of Irish history at the poetic symbolism surrounding the old mythological battles, praises Cuchulain, an "ancient" poet, for his "imagistic" language. Yeats praises Cuchulain for weaving around the Battle of Magh Tuireadh the mysterious aura that he himself will later weave around the battle of 1916. As the chief "scribe" of the Easter Rising, Yeats was to modern Ireland what the scribe Moelmuiri Mac Mic Duinn Na M-Bocht, sitting in his monastery at Clonmacnoise transcribing the Cuchulain sagas,[15] was to twelfth-century Ireland. The scribe is a man who preserves the sacred traditions of the past, and the more beautiful his illumination of those traditions, the more lasting will be their impact on the generations to come. Yeats's poems, and particularly his Cuchulain plays, which read like a series of illuminated portraits of a Celtic warrior, capture the tragic beauty of the Rising as surely as the endlessly spiralling designs in the *Book of Kells*[16] capture the restless imagination of the Celt.

The Mask of Cuchulain then was, in every sense of the word, the perfect

Mask for the men of 1916, for Cuchulain was both hero and poet and he reflects the perfect intertwining of passion and poetry, thought and action, that fascinated Yeats and the Irish rebels. The 1916 poets belonged to a cult of Cuchulain not only because Cuchulain was a hero but because, like them, he was a poet. He showed them that poets too can be great warriors if they are not afraid to choose their Antithetical Masks. Pearse and his comrades were not "natural" warriors like Cuchulain and we shall see in Chapter 2 that the Mask of the warrior was for them a most difficult Mask. Yet, when the time came, it was a Mask they chose courageously. To be sure, the poetic Mask adopted by the leaders of the Rebellion was a theatrical Mask, chosen deliberately by men with grand poetic visions and a great love for words, but it was a Mask worn on a stage where real bullets were fired and real blood was shed:

> It was bitterly cold at 3:30 a.m. even in May. Each prisoner had his hands tied behind his back. A cloth was placed over his eyes and a small piece of white paper about five inches square pinned to his coat over the heart. They died singly in the jail yard, standing with their backs to the wall. The volleys followed one another quickly.[17]

Yeats was horrified by the brutality of the executions, but deeply impressed by the courage of the men executed. In a letter to Lady Gregory dated 11 May 1916, Yeats writes: "The Dublin tragedy has been a great sorrow and anxiety. . . . I am trying to write a poem on the men executed: 'terrible beauty is born again.' I had no idea any public event could so deeply move me."[18] In 1938 when Yeats was writing "A General Introduction for My Work," the firing squads of 1916 and their connection with Cuchulain were still very much on his mind:

> Sometimes I am told in commendation, if the newspaper is Irish, in condemnation if English, that my movement perished under the firing squads of 1916; sometimes that those firing squads made our realistic movement possible. If that statement is true, and it is only so in part, for romance was everywhere receding, it is because in the imagination of Pearse and his fellow soldiers the Sacrifice of the Mass had found the Red Branch in the tapestry; they went out to die calling upon Cuchulain.[19]

Although Christians, the men had called upon the pagan hero of the Red Branch Knights, and Cuchulain had somehow become part of the Christian Mass. In a lecture given to the National Literary Society in Dublin in 1912, Pearse connected Cuchulain's heroic deeds, which he was later to dramatize in *The Defence of the Ford*, with Christ's redemptive sacrifice: "For the story of Cuchulain symbolises the redemption of many by a sinless God. . . . I do not mean that the *Tain* is a conscious allegory . . . it is like a retelling (or is it a foretelling?) of the story of Calvary."[20] Yeats was fascinated by the idea that

Christ and Cuchulain had merged in the imagination of the rebels, for Yeats's Christ was also a Celtic Christ, and, like Pearse, he held on to this image right up to his death:

> I am convinced that in two or three generations it will become generally known that the mechanical theory has no reality, that the natural and the supernatural are knit together, that to escape a dangerous fanaticism we must study a new science; at that moment Europeans may find something attractive in a Christ posed against a background not of Judaism but of Druidism, not shut off in dead history, but flowing, concrete, phenomenal.
> I was born into this faith, have lived it, and shall die in it; my Christ, a legitimate deduction from the Creed of St. Patrick as I think, is that Unity of Being Dante compared to a perfectly proportioned human body. . . .[21]

Yeats's Celtic Christ sounds much more like a Christianized Cuchulain than the traditional image of Christ presented to us by the Roman Church, for the Roman Church does not luxuriate in the beauty of Christ's physical body. In the early Irish Church, however, there was a great deal of emphasis on the beauty of Christ's body. According to Irish tradition, both Christ and Cuchulain have "perfectly proportioned" bodies, and their external beauty complements their "inner" perfection. Yeats, in "An Indian Monk," writes that Irish monks spread the doctrine that Christ was the most "beautiful" of men, and he adds: "Some Irish saint, whose name I have forgotten, sang, 'There is one among the birds that is perfect, one among the fish, one perfect among men.' "[22] He brings this up again in his unfinished novel, *The Speckled Bird*, where Michael declares that "Christ being the perfect man had perfect measurements."[23] And John Rhys, in *Celtic Heathendom*, observes that the Irish druids accepted Christ as the most "perfect" of druids.[24] Cuchulain, of course, was renowned for his exquisite "godlike" beauty. In the ancient sagas, the only fault the women of Ireland can find in him is that he is too "beautiful":

> When Cuchulain was growing out of his boyhood at Emain Macha, all the women of Ulster loved him for his skill in feats . . . for the sweetness of his speech, for the beauty of his face, for the loveliness of his looks, for all his gifts. He had the gift of divining . . . the gift of beauty. And all the faults they could find in him were that he was too daring, and that he was too beautiful.[25]

Through a confluence of pagan mythology and Christian sacrifice, Yeats felt Pearse and his followers had achieved in modern Dublin that perfect Druid-Christian unity that had existed in ancient Ireland. In Ireland, right through the Middle Ages, pagan rites and Christian rituals were everywhere intertwined. As R. A. S. Macalister, in *The Archeology of Ireland*, points out, for a long period of time Christianity in Ireland ran its destined course in a "chariot of pagan ritual." The noticeable absence of records of martyrdom in the history of early Irish Christianity, a fact which has frequently been commented upon by scholars, indicates that the Christianization of Ireland was not a matter of militant missionary evangelism, but of gradual, "almost imperceptible absorption and infiltration, throughout a long period of syncretism between the old cults and the new."[26] In the art which evolved from this Irish Insular Christianity, pagan and Christian symbols constantly consume each other, forming new and violent unities of "terrible beauty," which are reflected in the Cross of Cong, the *Book of Kells*, and in the Druid-Christian fabric of much of Yeats's own poetry. The Cross of Cong is a masterpiece of beauty and terror, for the exquisitely decorated cross rises majestically from the jaws of a giant beast (the pagan symbol of a former age). And on page after page of the magnificently illuminated *Book of Kells*, man and beast encircle and devour one another, trapped within the intricate interlacings of the Celtic circle. In Chapter 3, we shall see how Yeats, in his aesthetic adoption of the Cuchulain Mask in the Cuchulain play cycle, has captured both the spiritual passion and the dark virility of this art. Cuchulain, as he is depicted in the ancient sagas, is a strange blend of the animal energy and spiritual passion found in medieval Irish art. He is a splendid pagan renowned for his amazing virility and for his terrifying battle fury, which turns him momentarily into a beast.[27] Yet he is, at the same time, the very flower of chivalry, and is as romantic as any medieval Christian knight. Yeats preserves the "terrible beauty" of this synthesis in his Cuchulain plays.

When we consider the many different dimensions of Cuchulain's character as depicted in the Irish sagas, it becomes more and more apparent why Cuchulain was, for both Yeats and the 1916 rebels, an ideal national symbol. It also becomes apparent that any analysis of Yeats's use of Cuchulain as a symbol which fails to consider the multiple facets of Cuchulain's personality so evident in the Old Irish tales will fail, ultimately, to do justice to the rich complexity of the Cuchulain symbol as utilized by Yeats. Although Yeats added his own coloring to the Cuchulain symbol, the sagas provided him with a powerful ready-made archetype that already contained all of the intriguing complexity that Yeats admired. Most importantly, the metamorphic personality of Cuchulain, so vividly portrayed in the *Tain*, offered to Yeats a perfect example of the dynamic duality which would later find expression in his doctrine of the Mask. This duality will be discussed in depth in Chapter 2, along with a discussion of Yeats's concept of the Mask and its connection with Irish mythology and fairylore.

The reverence with which Irish Christians, right through the Middle Ages, treated their pagan ancestors like Cuchulain should be examined, for the same Insular attitudes that existed in medieval Ireland, were evident among the poet-leaders of the Rising. Aodh de Blacam's words regarding Irish Insular Christianity are especially illuminating:

> We must observe carefully the difference here suggested between the treatment of pagan lore by Irish writers and the treatment of Classical mythology by the Church on the Continent. In the Roman Empire, paganism meant the vices of a decadent civilisation. The Church could allow no truck with the memory of gods whose names gave names to horrid sins. The centuries in the desert, and the suspension of Classical learning, were necessary to purge the nations of the Empire from corruption. Paganism in Ireland rather meant nature unlighted by revelation. . . . Certainly Christianity caused no set-back to Irish imaginative life; for the great stories . . . gain final dramatic point from Christian additions. The clergy, too, were the transcribers and preservers of the heroic tales.[28]

Yeats refers again and again to the unique qualities of the Celtic Church as opposed to the Church on the Continent. He celebrates that time in ancient Ireland when "the umbilical cord which united Christianity to the ancient world had not yet been cut," and "Christ was still the half-brother of Dionysus"[29] and Cuchulain. Yeats writes that in ancient Ireland "a man just tonsured by the Druids could learn from the nearest Christian neighbour to sign himself with the Cross without sense of incongruity, nor would his children acquire that sense."[30] Many of the attitudes and practices of the Irish Insular Church that Yeats admired so much were, however, looked upon as being almost "heretical" by Rome:

> The early Irish Church never lapsed into formal heresy, but there were always curious ideas abroad that in Rome, or indeed anywhere else in Christendom, would be looked upon as somewhat strange. . . . A certain number of these had to do with the existence of a strong and arrogant nationalistic spirit.[31]

This "strong and arrogant nationalistic spirit" was very much alive in 1916 when the Christian rebels invoked the spirit of the pagan warrior Cuchulain, and they too were called heretics because of their strange theology.[32] Those individuals who saw Pearse's linking of Cuchulain with Christ as bizarre and neurotic failed to recognize that Pearse was acting within the Irish Insular tradition. Moreover, within that tradition, Pearse could look for authority to St. Patrick himself, who, like Pearse, had called on the spirit of Cuchulain to help Ireland. The Old Irish tale "Cuchulain's Demon Chariot" tells how St. Patrick called up the spirit of Cuchulain to help in the conversion of Laegaire, king of Ireland, to Christianity.[33] It is clear that an awareness of the Irish Insular Christian tradition and its far-reaching effects on Irish art, literature, and nationalism will enrich our understanding of Yeats's political poetry and the complex imaginative forces at work behind the Easter Rising.

It will help us to understand why in Ireland an ancient "pagan" mythology had, in an extraordinary way, influenced the birth of a modern "Catholic" nation, and why Yeats saw this phenomenon as a cause for great celebration:

> Come gather round me, players all:
> Come praise Nineteen-Sixteen
> Those from the pit and gallery
> Or from the painted scene
> That fought in the Post Office
> Or round the City Hall.
>
> ("Three Songs to the One Burden," 55–60)

When Yeats depicts the battle in the Post Office as a "painted scene," he is accurately describing the strange and beautiful movements of aristocratic warrior poets upon a modern stage, for that is certainly how the poet rebels saw themselves. We shall see in Chapter 2 that Padraic Pearse, Thomas MacDonagh and Joseph Mary Plunkett, the poet leaders who masterminded the Rebellion, had their own concept of Mask and Image. Their poems and plays reveal that Yeats's perception of them as "players" in a ritual drama of Masks is remarkably close to their perception of themselves.[34] These poets chose to impose upon the sterility of modern Dublin a "painted scene" of the heroic pagan past. And if this "scene" seems strangely artificial in a non-heroic age, Yeats still saw great beauty in its antique art, created as it was out of human blood:

> "But where can we draw water,"
> Said Pearse to Connolly,
> "When all the wells are parched away?"
> O plain as plain can be
> There's nothing but our own red blood
> Can make a right Rose Tree."
>
> ("The Rose Tree," 13–18)

The Rose Tree reflects the same kind of terror and beauty as the Mask of Cuchulain. It is a symbol of "terrible beauty" because in Ireland it required human sacrifice in order to bloom. The exquisite petals of Yeats's Rose have not been created by the delicate brush strokes of ascetic artists far removed from the chaos of life, but by poets who shed real blood to bring it to life again. And while ancient Ireland may equal Byzantium in Yeats's imagination, the Mask of Cuchulain, like the Rose, has not been forged out of "hammered gold and gold enamelling" to stand in stylized perfection before a "gong-tormented" world, but is a Mask adopted by living men in a real rebellion. Both the Rose and the Mask of Cuchulain are symbols that stem from the passion which is itself part of "the fury and the mire of human veins" and, during the Rising, the splendor of that passion made even Byzantine domes seem insignificant. We shall see later that the image of the Rose, like the stone symbol in "Easter 1916" and the Cuchulain plays, is one of those multifaceted Irish symbols that Yeats masterfully uses in his poetry. These symbols are rooted in a landscape that is both pagan and Christian, and Yeats stresses the importance of such Irish symbols:

> I could not endure, however, an international art, picking stories and symbols where it pleased. Might I not, with health and good luck to aid me, create some new Prometheus Unbound; Patrick or Columcille, Oisin or Finn, in Prometheus' stead; and, instead of Caucasus, Cro-Patrick or Ben Bulben?[35]

But Yeats also knew that, no matter how beautiful these Irish symbols were, they needed human passion to bring them to life. In his prose draft of the poem "The Statues," which refers to Cuchulain and the Irish Rebellion, Yeats writes that "only passion sees God," and the poem stresses passion over abstract knowledge: "Empty eyeballs knew / That knowledge increases unreality, that / Mirror on mirror mirrored is all the show" (20–22). But passion, Yeats writes in the poem, can bring life to the coldness of art:

> But boys and girls, pale from the imagined love
> Of solitary beds, knew what they were,
> That passion could bring character enough,
> And pressed at midnight in some public place
> Live lips upon a plummet-measured face.
>
> ("The Statues," 4–8)

In the Easter Rebellion, the rebel poets gave new life to Ireland's ancient symbols and icons by passionately endorsing those symbols with their blood. Thomas MacDonagh, one of the poets executed in 1916, knew well what Yeats meant about the futility of poetic words and images without passion, and he writes about this in his poem "Inscriptions of Ireland":

> What of my careful ways of speech?
> What are my cold words to the heart
> That lives in man? They cannot reach
> One passion simpler than their art.
>
> Though silence be the meed of death
> In dust of death a soul doth burn:
> Poet, rekindled by thy breath
> Joy flames within her funeral urn.[36]

Knowing that only death could express "One passion simpler than their art," Pearse and his followers gave permanent form to their artistic visions by surrendering their lives. As William Irwin Thompson observes, they made out of Irish history a work of art.[37] And Yeats, in his poetry on the Rising, created out of their passion a national icon. Richard Loftus, in his article "Yeats and the Easter Rising: A Study in Ritual," notes that Yeats "elevates the insurrectionaries to a mythological world where the battle is identical with the dance, where swords flash but never strike home, where every movement has symbolic meaning."[38]

For Yeats, the poetic symbolism of the Rebellion and its connection with Irish mythology confirmed his belief in an unbroken legacy of Irish thought rooted in a "great tapestry" which contained Cuchulain and all the other heroes of ancient Ireland. In "A General Introduction for My Work," Yeats writes:

> Behind all Irish history hangs a great tapestry, even Christianity had to accept it and be itself pictured there. Nobody looking at its dim folds can say where Christianity begins and Druidism ends. . . . That tapestry filled the scene at the birth of modern Irish literature, it is there in the Synge of *The Well of the Saints*, in James Stephens, and in Lady Gregory throughout, in all of George Russell that did not come from the Upanishads, and in all but my later poetry.[39]

According to Yeats, every aspect of Irish life and thought has been formed by this great tapestry—this Druid-Christian matrix—and his poetry on the Rising is inextricably bound up with his ideas on the great tapestry and its powerful influence on the Irish imagination. Cuchulain, the Rose, the Stone, and all the other symbols of "terrible beauty" which are part of the landscape of Yeats's poems and plays connected with the Rising lie within the "dim folds" of that tapestry. The Mask of Cuchulain, the central symbol of the Rising itself as it emerges in the rich threads of that tapestry, embodies the "terrible beauty" of Ireland herself, her age-old traditions, her fatalistic yet joyful attitude towards love and death, her mordant lyrical passion, and her "turbulent, indomitable reaction against the despotism of fact,"[40]—all those things which brought about the "troubled ecstasy" of "Easter 1916": "All changed, changed utterly: / A terrible beauty is born" (15–16).

This study, therefore, considers the Mask of Cuchulain not only as an individual Mask, but as a composite Mask of these various elements, and ultimately, as part of a richly woven and complex cultural ideal. Seamus Heaney once wrote that he saw poems as "elements of continuity with the aura and authenticity of archeological finds. . . ."[41] He describes poetry as a dig, "a dig for finds that end up being plants."[42] Heaney's view of poetry is particularly relevant to this study, for this study is a "dig" which penetrates the Masks, Images and motifs that formed the background of the Rising, in an attempt to understand the more ancient designs of the Druid-Christian tapestry to which they are tied. This study, therefore, will look deep within the folds of the great tapestry and will go back to what Yeats describes as "the aboriginal ice" behind Irish legend, to discover the "kind" of imagination and the kind of culture that created heroes like Cuchulain—heroes who sum up the imaginative history of their race in all its fatal beauty. It is essential to do this because Yeats, believing in the unbroken continuity of the Irish imagination, held that the same imagination which sent Cuchulain out to fight the armies of Queen Maeve also sent the rebels out to fight the British, that the imagination which created Cuchulain was present in 1916 when the rebels went out to die: "Who thought Cuchulain till it seemed / He stood where they stood."[43]

ii

In the preface to *Cuchulain of Muirthemne,* Yeats has much to say about the kind of imagination that Pearse and his followers had inherited from the ancient Irish, an imagination which provoked them into a fatal search for an elusive beauty. Yeats writes that the Irish storyteller, unlike the Norse and other non-Celtic storytellers, was not interested in reality. His imagination delighted in taking flight to Tir na Nog (Land of Youth), which Yeats believed "is as near to the country people today as it was to Cuchulain and his companions. His belief in its nearness cherished in its turn the lyrical temper, which is always athirst for an emotion, a beauty which cannot be found in its perfection upon earth, or only for a moment."[44] Pearse and his comrades, "athirst" for such an emotion, "gave themselves up to imagination as if to a lover"[45] and like the ancient Irish poets "believed or half-believed in the historical reality of their wildest imaginations."[46] In 1916, the lover, of course, was Cathleen Ni Houlihan—Ireland herself—and the price of surrender to her was death. In "The Celtic Element in Literature," Yeats points out that in ancient Ireland love was held to be a fatal sickness, and he adds that "there is a love poem in the Love Songs of Connacht that is like a death-cry."[47] The following lines which Yeats quotes from the poem reflect this erotic fatalism:

> My love, O she is my love,
> the woman who is most for destroying me,
> dearer is she for making me ill
> than the woman who would be for making me well.
> She is my treasure, O she is my treasure,
> the woman of the grey eyes
> A woman who would not lay a hand under my head.
> . . . She is my love, O she is my love,
> the woman who left no strength in me;
> a woman who would not raise a stone at my tomb. . . .[48]

Although the intertwining of love and death was a common motif in Western literature which flowered in the courtly love circles of the Middle

Ages and has been brilliantly analyzed by Denis de Rougement,[49] it remained no more than a literary convention. In Ireland, however, the poetic tradition which reflected the love-death motif existed not merely as a literary convention, but had powerful nationalistic implications. From the dawn of Irish history, Ireland has been personified as a woman and was often referred to as a beautiful rose. Through the centuries of British occupation, Irish poet patriots wrote beautiful love poems to this fatal rose declaring their willingness to die for her, and often proved their sincerity by actually dying for her. The first elegy that comes down to us from the dim past of Milesian Ireland is a poem which reflects the love-death motif. The poem tells of how Fail, the wife of Lugai, nephew of Milesius, saw her husband naked while bathing and, thinking him a stranger, died of shame. Her husband wrote her "death-song," which was the first elegy ever composed in Ireland by a Milesian. The meter and rhyme-sounds of the Old Irish poem are reproduced in the English version below:

> Sate we sole, in cliff-bower
>   Chill winds shower
> I tremble yet—shock of dread
>   Sped death's power.
> The tale I tell:fate has felled
>   Fail most fine.
>
> She a man, bare, beheld,
>   In sun shine,
> Shock of death, death's dread power,
>   Lowered fell fate,
> Bare I came, hence her shame,
>   Stilled she sate.[50]

As we shall see later, the word *Fail*, combined with the Irish word *Inis* (island) to become one of the common names of Ireland—Inisfail. Yeats, noting the continuity of the love-death tradition, quotes the following lines from the song, "Roisin Dubh" (Little Black Rose):

> The Erne shall be in strong flood
> The hills shall be torn down
> And the sea shall have red waves
> And blood shall be spilled, and every
> mountain valley and moor shall be on high,
> Before you shall perish, my little Black Rose.[51]

The "little Black Rose" is Ireland personified, and her "terrible beauty" is associated with death. The rose is black with the dried blood of young men who through the centuries have given up their lives to make her free. In 1916, another generation of young men only too eager to surrender to her seductive lure sacrificed themselves upon her altar: "There's nothing but our own red blood / Can make a right Rose Tree" (17–18). Yeats has much to say about the rose as a religious and literary symbol in Ireland:

> I have read somewhere that a stone engraved with a Celtic god, who holds what looks like a Rose in one hand, has been found somewhere. . . . One may feel pretty certain that the ancient Celts associated the Rose with Eire, or Fotla, or Banba—goddesses who gave their names to Ireland—for such symbols are not suddenly adopted or invented, but come out of mythology. . . . One finds the Rose in the Irish poets, sometimes as a religious symbol, as in the phrase, "the Rose of Friday," meaning the Rose of austerity, in a Gaelic poem in Dr. Hyde's "Religious Songs of Connacht," and I think as a symbol of woman's beauty in the Gaelic song, "Roisin Dubh"; and a symbol of Ireland in Mangan's adaption of "Roisin Dubh," "My Dark Rosaleen," and in Mr. Aubrey de Vere's "The Little Black Rose."[52]

The Rose, then, is deeply imbedded in Yeats's ancient Irish tapestry, and is woven from both the pagan and Christian threads of that tapestry. It is one of Yeats's fertile images—"Those images that yet / Fresh images beget" ("Byzantium," 38–39). Yeats, in modern times, revitalized the symbol of the rose, blending it with his occult philosophy and exploiting its many dimensions throughout his poetry. Like a Druid poet of old, he used his poetic powers to preserve the sacred mystery of the rose and to draw young men to the poetic service of the rose once again: "Come near, I would before my time to go / Sing of Old Eire and her ancient ways: / Red Rose, proud Rose, sad Rose of all my days" ("The Rose," 22–24). The poets of 1916 eagerly took up Yeats's call to "sing of old Eire and the ancient ways" and Pearse acknowledged Yeats's enormous influence on himself and his comrades:

> We cannot forget that he has spent his life in an endeavor to free our ideas of foreign thought, or that it was through his writings many of us made our first acquaintance with our early traditions and literature. He has never ceased to work for Ireland.[53]

Yeats not only held up the ancient "traditions and literature" of Ireland for all to see, but he showed how hauntingly beautiful those traditions and that literature could be:

> The great emotions of love, terror, and friendship must alone remain untroubled by the moon in that world, which is still the world of the Irish country-people, who do not open their eyes very wide at the most miraculous change, at the most hidden enchantment. Its events, and things, and people are wild, and are like unbroken horses, that are so much more beautiful than horses that have learned to run between shafts.[54]

To die for the Black Rose was an integral part of those ancient traditions, and the poems and actions of the 1916 poets clearly represent the continuation of those traditions. Joseph Plunkett's poem "The Little Black Rose shall be Red at Last," for example, is both a love poem to Ireland and his fiancee, and at the same time a death-cry. Written in highly erotic imagery, the poem forecasts his own death in the Easter Rebellion:

> Because we share our sorrows and our joys
> And all your dear and intimate thoughts are mine
> We shall not fear the trumpets and the noise
> Of battle, for we know our dreams divine,
> And when my heart is pillowed on your heart
> And ebb and flowing of their passionate flood
> Shall beat in concord love through every part
> of brain and body, when at last the blood
> O'erleaps the final barrier to find
> Only one source wherein to spend its strength.
> And we two lovers, long but one in mind
> And soul, are made one only flesh at length;
> Praise God if this my blood fulfills the doom
> When you, dark rose, shall redden into bloom.[55]

Plunkett's blood, like the blood of Cuchulain, shall help Ireland to blossom rather than bring forth any human life: "When you, dark rose, shall redden into bloom." The young poet's last moments can be described as a dark epiphany of love and death, a perfect reflection of the Irish poetic tradition he so passionately embraced. Just minutes before his execution, Plunkett married his fiancee Grace Gifford in a small candle-lit chapel filled with armed troops.[56] Immediately following the ceremony, he was led to his death. Thus, like many of the heroes in the Old Irish romances, Plunkett turns from the arms of a living bride to Ireland, the more demanding bride of death.

Plunkett's actions just before his death remind us of the actions of the young man in Yeats's play *Cathleen Ni Houlihan*. In the play, Cathleen (Ireland), played by Maud Gonne, lures young Michael away from his bride on the eve of his wedding. "Many a man had died for love of me" she declares and sings of the golden-haired Donough that was hanged in Galway:

> I will go cry with the woman,
> For yellow-haired Donough is dead,
> With a hempen rope for a neck-cloth,
> And a white cloth on his head.[57]

Plunkett, like Michael in the play, will sacrifice his bride and choose death so that Cathleen's "four beautiful green fields"[58] may be restored to her. These fields represent the four provinces of Ireland—Ulster, Munster, Leinster, and Connacht—and today in Ireland the song "Four Green Fields" is still a very popular ballad. In Ireland, as Yeats himself has said, "the past is always alive."[59] The play enflamed the hearts of many young Irish men and women, and Pearse declared that it was "the most beautiful play that has been written in Ireland in our time."[60] Stephen Gwynn, after seeing the play, wrote in *Irish Literature and Drama:* "The effect of *Cathleen Ni Houlihan* on me was that I went home asking myself if such plays should be produced unless one was prepared for people to go out to shoot and be shot."[61] Yeats, knowing well the effect of passionate words on the Irish imagination, felt that he did indeed bear some responsibility for the events of 1916. In his poem "The Man and the Echo" written the year before his death, he is still agonizing over that terrible burden:

> All that I have said and done,
> Now that I am old and ill,
> Turns into a question still
> I lie awake night after night
> And never get the answers right.
> Did that play of mine send out
> Certain men the English shot?
>
> (6–12)

Plunkett, one of those "men the English shot" shared Yeats's romantic dream for Ireland but felt that writing poetry was not enough to achieve that dream. Like the Knight of St. John in Yeats's story *Out of the Rose,* Plunkett felt that he must prove his love for Ireland by "dying in the service of the Rose."[62] And throughout his poetry love and death are everywhere intertwined. The following lines from his poem "I love you with every Breath" reflect this fatal union:

> I love you with every breath
> I make you sing like thunder birds
> Give you my life—you give me death.[63]

And in his poem "My Lady has the Grace of Death" he writes: "She took my sword from her side all bloody / And she died for love."[64] Here death occurs at the moment of sexual consummation; and, in his poem "There is no Deed I would not Dare," he again resorts to sword imagery to reflect both his fear of and attraction to the lethal aspects of sexual union:

> But I do love you and I know
> Nor any deed nor difficult quest
> To try to compass, that would show
> The fire that burns within my breast
> I cannot draw the dazzling blade
> My body sheathes, Love's splendid sword,

> Lest you be blinded and dismayed,
> To silence fall my wounded word.[65]

Pearse, like Plunkett, sees death in love and love in death. In his poem "A Song for Mary Magadeline," he creates a strange religious/erotic symmetry where even Christ seems to have died for a woman:

> O woman of the snowy side,
> Many a lover hath lain with thee,
> Yet left thee sad at the morning tide,
> But thy lover Christ shall comfort thee.
> O woman that no lover's kiss
> (Tho' many a kiss was given thee)
> Could slake thy love, is it not for this
> The Hero Christ shall die for thee?[66]

In another poem, Pearse speaks of death itself as a lover:

> I have made my heart clean tonight
> As a woman might clean her house
> Ere her lover come to visit her:
> O Lover, pass not by.[67]

Like Pearse and Plunkett, Thomas MacDonagh writes as though his entire life has been an odyssey towards the Rose of Death:

> Three things through love I see
> Sorrow and sin and death
> And my mind reminding me
> That this doom I breathe with my breath
>
> But sweeter than violin or lute
> Is my love, and she left me behind
> I wish that all music were mute
> And I to my beauty were blind.[68]

To capture the "terrible beauty" of the Ireland he was to die for in 1916, MacDonagh returns to the traditional symbol of the rose:

> O Rose of Grace! O rare wild flower
> Whose seeds are sent on the wings of Light!
> O secret rose, our doom our dower,
> Black with the passion of our night.[69]

The poets of 1916 wrote and died in a tradition as old as Ireland herself— they employed ancient Masks and symbols to reflect their sacrifice and, according to Yeats, "stepped back into the tapestry" to become potent symbols for future generations:

> If Irish literature goes on as my generation planned it, it may do something to keep the "Irishry" living, nor will the work of the realists hinder, nor the figures they imagine, nor those described in memoirs of the revolution. These last especially, like certain great political predecessors, Parnell, Swift, Lord Edward, have stepped back into the tapestry.[70]

Nor has this tradition of poetic sacrifice died out since Easter 1916. In the Ireland of 1981, a young man named Bobby Sands turned once again to the "terrible beauty" of Yeats's great tapestry for his own poetic symbols, and he too, like his predecessors in 1916, goes out to die calling upon the heroes of ancient Ireland. He mourns because "the blood still lies on Kerry's roads / Unwashed by winds of old / The hares cross lonely, barren ways / Where once columns tramped the night."[71] And he asks "Who cares for Kerry's lonely graves / The King of Cashel's gone to Clare."[72] Chastising modern Irish poets for ignoring the real suffering in the North, he writes: "The men of Art have lost their heart / They dream within their dreams."[73] To express the apathy of modern Ireland, he returns to the symbol of the rose. In his poem "The Sleeping Rose," he writes that "the Rose of Munster's dead" and "will not bloom again"[74] until the men of Munster shed their blood. This poem clearly echoes Yeats's poem "The Rose Tree," where Connolly tells Pearse that "nothing but our own red blood / Can make a right Rose Tree." Sands, of course, was familiar with Yeats's poetry on the Rising, and, by the time of Sand's death in 1981, Yeats had taken his rightful place in the great Irish tapestry, enshrined forever in the mythology of the Rising that he himself had helped to create:

> While still I may, I write for you
> The love I lived, the dream I knew.
> From our birthday, until we die
> Is but the winking of an eye; . . .
> I cast my heart into my rhymes,
> That you may know in the coming times,
> May know how my heart went with them
> After the red-rose-bordered hem.
> ("To Ireland in the Coming Times," 33–36, 45–48)

Bobby Sands, like Yeats and the men of 1916, spent his life enthralled by that "red-rose-bordered hem." Although his poems were not great, the passions that lay behind them were, and, like the men of 1916, he endorsed his poetry with his blood. He was only twenty-seven years old when he died on hunger strike in the H-Block of Long Kesh, and he represents the continuation of an ancient tradition of "terrible beauty" stretching back to the days of

Cuchulain, a tradition of dying for the fatal beauty of the "Black Rose." "Our mother ground," Seamus Heaney writes in his poem "Kinship," "is sour with the blood / of her faithful."[75] Heaney describes Ireland as "an insatiable bride / Sword-swallower / casket, midden / floe of history"[76] and concludes the poem with the following lines: "how the goddess swallows / our love and terror."[77] Despite the insatiable nature of that bride, Heaney, like Yeats and the poets of 1916, falls prey to her beauty:

> I love this turf-face
> its black incisions,
> the cooped secrets
> of process and ritual;
>
> I love the spring
> off the ground,
> each bank a gallows drop,
> each open pool
> the unstopped mouth
> of an urn, a moon-drinker,
> by the naked eye.[78]

In this land of "cooped secrets" and "black incisions," of "process and ritual," to die well is to create art. Even the "Old Woman of Beare" who has lost her beauty and her youth can make poetry out of her death:

> The Old Woman of Beare am I
> Who once was beautiful.
> Now all I know is how to die.
> I'll do it well.[79]

iii

Andre Malraux, in *Antimemoires,* writes that every culture, visible or invisible, "is impelled by its own conception of death."[80] This is certainly true of Ireland where the very landscape with its megalithic tombs, prehistoric burial mounds, and druidic ruins creates a strange poetry of death. Seamus Heaney, lured by the haunting beauty of these ancient burial chambers, writes in his poem "Funeral Rites": "I would restore / the great chambers of Boyne / prepare a sepulchre / under the cupmarked stones."[81] Since Yeats and the poets of 1916 get caught up in this poetry of death, we must step back into that tapestry again to trace the origins of certain attitudes towards death which reach their culmination in both the Rising itself and in Yeats's treatment of it.

There is a very interesting Old Irish poem written about A.D. 900, which expresses views of fatalism and destiny current in Ireland from an early period. Some preliminary comment about the background of the poem will help the modern reader.

The Irish held a strange belief that every individual was alloted at birth three "sods" or spots: the "sod of birth," the "sod of death," and the "sod of burial."[82] Each sod was predestined, and the sod of burial (as distinct from the sod of death) was the predestined place of the resurrection of the body on the Last Day. The sod of death was conceived as a special piece of earth somewhere in the world upon which a man would one day step, and that moment of contact would be the moment of his death. The sod of death seems to lure everyone on, and belief in it still exists in Irish folklore. A common type of folktale tells how a man, having discovered his sod of death, threw it to the bottom of the sea. But miraculously, at the predestined moment, the sod would appear beneath the foot of the man who was about to die.[83] An excellent example of this belief exists in the *Tain*. When Cuchulain blames Queen Maeve for forcing Ferdia to fight against him and tries to get Ferdia to give up the fight before he meets his death, Ferdia replies: "O Cuchulain, giver of wounds, true hero, every man must come in the end to the sod where his last grave shall be."[84] Even the 1916 poets refer to the sod in their poems. Plunkett, just one year before his execution writes of the duty of the Irish to "guard the sod / That holds their father's funeral urn."[85]

Maura Carney's translation of a passage from a statement written in Irish in 1945 by a sixty-eight-year-old Irish speaker from Doolin, County Clare, expresses the beliefs of the local people concerning fate and destiny:

> I wish to mention the belief the old people had that it was laid out for a person from the time the crown of his head came into the world where his place of death (fod a bhais) was. For this person it was laid out that for him, or for her, the side of the road would be as a sod of death, for another the middle of the field, or out on the brown mountain, or in the loneliness of the wood, or—God save us from danger! a person could have as a sod of death a violent death. I remember when a poor girl from this town fell down a terrible cliff over there a dozen years ago, what an old neighbour, no longer living for many a day, said. There were droves of people from the towns around present, everywhere taking the full of their eyes fearfully of the poor dead thing who was thrown there on a fissure in the cliff hundreds of feet from the top. This person and that were trying to ease in some way the torment of the girl's father, but what the old man I mentioned had to say when he looked down at the dreadful sight was, "Twas her sod of death that was there (Se fod a bais do bhi ann)."[86]

James Carney notes that the old man's phrase used over the dead girl's body, which literally in Anglo-Irish idiom means, "Twas her sod of death that was in it," shows precisely the same thinking as the tenth-century poem, several verses of which are presented below in English verse translation:

I walk the lonely mountain road,
  O King of Suns, and darkest glen,
no nearer death, though I be alone,
  than fared I with three thousand men.

 . . . .

It is no paltry little man
  that can take my life away,
only the Maker of earth and sky,
  the Shaper of the summer day.

Signs stop me not from setting out
  Did someone sneeze? for my last breath
will be when foot compulsively
  treads the awaiting sod of death.

I fear no more to walk alone
  let the world which shaped, gave me birth,
take not untimely back but wait
  for nut-ripe falling to the earth.

The lad who risks his gleaming skin
  in yon ford opposing might,
must he, then, be nearer death
  than the skulker from the fight?

 . . . .

Alas! Alas! Avoiding death
  takes too much time and too much care,
and then, at very end of all,
  he catches each one unaware.

May God and ranks of angels nine
  be ever watchful over me
from terror, from caverns of white death
  protecting, bearing company.[87]

According to the poem, death with all its terror comes to each individual in a very different way, for each one of us has his own unique "sod of death." This gives to each person's death a certain grandeur. There is nothing accidental or arbitrary about it, for the "King of Suns" himself has created at our birth the individual design of our death. Since our death is already fated, the poet advises, we should embrace life passionately like "the lad who risks his gleaming skin / in yon ford opposing might" and not waste precious time trying to avoid death: "Alas! Alas! Avoiding death / takes too much time and too much care / And then, at very end of all, / he catches each one unaware." Like Cuchulain, "whose life is vehement and full of pleasure, as though he always remembered that it was to be soon over,"[88] we should make poetry and drama of both our life and our death, by uniting our conscious will with the will of fate or God—and when it is time for us to die, we must, like the

Old Wife of Beare, "do it well." Like the great King Loiguire, we must look death in the face. King Loiguire was the last pagan king of Ireland and he was buried at Tara in an upright position facing Leinster in full battle attire, "for he was ever an enemy of the men of Leinster."[89] P. M. Joyce, in *A Social History of Ancient Ireland*, points out that the dead were often buried standing up fully armed as if staring defiantly into death.[90] Yeats, approaching his own death, wrote of this mode of burial in his poem, "The Black Tower":

> There in the tomb stand the dead upright,
> But winds come up from the shore:
> They shake when the winds roar,
> Old bones upon the mountain shake.
>
> (7–10)

Pearse and his fellow soldiers—modern warriors embracing ancient ideals——go to their death like these kings of old. The following lines from Plunkett's poem "This Heritage to the Race of Kings" seem to forecast the "terrible beauty" of the Easter Rising:

> This heritage of the race of kings
> Their children and their children's seed
> Have wrought their prophecies in deed
> Of terrible and splendid things.[91]

The terrible and splendid things that Plunkett wrote about were the things that have made up the history of Ireland—violence, bloodshed and death, and the splendid poetry and song that has grown out of that blood:

> Irish poets, learn your trade,
> Sing whatever is well made. . . .
> Sing the lords and ladies gay
> That were beaten into the clay
> Through seven heroic centuries;
> Cast your mind on other days
> That we in coming days may be
> Still the indomitable Irishry.
>
> ("Under Ben Bullen," 5:1–2, 11–16)

When Yeats refers to the Irish as "indomitable," he appears to be consciously repeating the term used by Roger Casement as a prisoner in the dock when he was sentenced to death. Casement spoke of the "indomitable persistency" of the Irish in their struggle for freedom. The following is an excerpt from Casement's speech:

The cause that begets this indomitable persistency, the faculty of preserving through centuries of misery the remembrance of lost liberty—this surely is the noblest cause ever man strove for, ever lived for, ever died for. If this be the cause I stand here today indicted for and convicted of sustaining, then I stand in a goodly company and a right noble succession.[92]

Casement was the last one to be executed in 1916. He was hanged at Pentonville Prison, London, on 3 August 1916, following trial and conviction under a medieval statute written in Norman French defining high treason outside the realm. His defence was that he was an Irishman. Yeats saw Casement as a heroic individual who faced death as unflinchingly as those knights in "The Black Tower." The lines "Sing the lords and ladies gay / That were beaten into clay" were taken from a beautiful Irish poem written around the seventeenth century by an anonymous poet and translated by Frank O'Connor. The name of the poem is "Kilcash." Kilcash was the stately home of a branch of the Butler family, and the poem was one of Yeats's favorites. The poem links the fall of the aristocratic Irish house with the death of Ireland herself under British rule. As if to prove his theory about the unbroken continuity of the Gaelic tradition, Yeats, in "Under Ben Bulben," has placed next to the words of a seventeenth-century Irish poet, the words of a modern Irish patriot who is about to die. And although three hundred years had passed since "Kilcash" was written, Yeats, the writer of that poem, and Roger Casement shared an equally passionate desire to restore to Ireland her lost beauty—her "lords and ladies gay / That were beaten into the clay / Through seven heroic centuries."

The modern Irish poet Brendan Kennelly, who, like Yeats, believes in the unbroken continuity of the Irish imagination, maintains that in the field of literature Gaelic and Anglo-Irish combine to create a distinctively "Irish" tradition. Kennelly maintains that legends, myths, themes, rhythms, and ideas are not like social groups or political parties.[93] They do not thrive on an identity based on a sense of separateness. Rather "they fertilize and enrich each other constantly and deliberately in order to create new legends, myths, themes, rhythms, and ideas."[94] Kennelly sees Yeats's achievement alone as sufficient to justify the fusion of Gaelic and Anglo-Irish into a single solid tradition:

> An outstanding example of the fertilizing influence of one mode of thought and expression on another is the way in which Yeats took the dust-covered figures of Cuchulain, Conchubar, Maeve and others and proved how totally adequate these products of an ancient mythology were to express the immense complexity of life in the twentieth century.[95]

Kennelly concludes that, while history nearly always sundered Irish from Anglo-Irish, "the imagination has nearly always brought them closer together so that now, in retrospect, the cultures they both produced may be seen as a compact imaginative unity."[96]

If we look back over the "seven heroic centuries" mentioned by Yeats in "Under Ben Bulben," we find this "imaginative unity" particularly evident in the numerous Irish poems and legends about death. Irish art, Yeats writes, is often at its greatest when it is most extravagant.[97] And nowhere is this extravagance more evident than in its passionate lamentations of death. In "The Celtic Element in Literature," Yeats writes that the Old Irish always loved tales about death and parting, and delighted in "wild and beautiful lamentations":[98]

Life was so weighed down by the emptiness of the great forests and by the mystery of all things, and by the greatness of its own desires, and, as I think, by the loneliness of much beauty; and seemed so little and so fragile and so brief, that nothing could be more sweet in the memory than a tale that ended in death and parting, and than a wild and beautiful lamentation. Men did not mourn merely because their beloved was married to another, . . . , for such mourning believes that life might be happy were it different, and is therefore the less mourning, but because they had been born and must die with their great thirst unslaked.[99]

A wonderful eighteenth century poem entitled "The Lament for Art O'Leary," is one of those "wild and beautiful lamentations" of which Yeats speaks. Art O'Leary was murdered in Carriganima, County Cork, in 1773 for refusing to sell his famous mare to a Protestant named Morris for five pounds. Catholics were not permitted by British law to possess a horse of greater value than this. The lament was written in Irish by Art O'Leary's wife, Eileen, and was translated by Frank O'Connor. Although a reading of the entire poem is necessary in order to appreciate its beauty, the following verses capture something of the extravagant passion and heroic courage we find in many Irish poems concerning death:

> I clapped my hands,
> And off at a gallop;
> I never lingered
> Till I found you lying
> By a little furze-bush
> Without pope or bishop
> Or priest or cleric
> One prayer to whisper
> But an old, old woman,
> And her cloak about you,
> And your blood in torrents—
> Art O'Leary—
> I did not wipe it off
> I drank it from my palms.
>
> My love and my delight
> Stand up now beside me,

> And let me lead you home
> Until I make a feast,
> And I will roast the meat
> And send for company
> And call the harpers in,
> And I shall make your bed
> Of soft and snowy sheets
> And blankets dark and rough
> To warm the beloved limbs
> An autumn blast has chilled.
>
> . . . .
>
> But cease your weeping now,
> Women of the soft, wet eyes
> Till Art O'Leary drink
> Ere he go to the dark school—
> Not to learn music or song
> But to prop the earth and the stone. [100]

By surrounding her husband's death with so much beauty and so much passion, O'Leary's wife achieves mastery over it. She may mourn intensely, but she will also "make a feast," "roast the meat," "And call the harpers in." Defiantly railing against the despotism of death, she tells the women to stop their weeping until her husband has his last drink before he goes off to "the dark school" where he will "prop the earth and the stone." She refuses to allow death to diminish him and, rather than turning aside from the physical aspects of his death, she voluptuously immerses herself in them: "And your blood in torrents / Art O'Leary / I did not wipe it off / I drank it from my palms."

Two centuries later, "The O'Rahilly," mortally wounded in the Easter Rising, reflects the same heroic passion as Eileen O'Leary. Although he died alone, stretched under a doorway in Henry Street, he never forgets for a moment that he is one of the "indomitable Irishry," one of that glorious "race of kings." His last gesture is sheer poetry—with his own blood, he writes his epitaph on the door above his head. Yeats writes of this in his poem "The O'Rahilly":

> What remains to sing about
> But of the death he met
> Stretched under a doorway
> Somewhere off Henry Street;
> They that found him found upon
> The door above his head
> "Here died the O'Rahilly.
> R.I.P." writ in blood.

(28–35)

And just as Eileen O'Leary calls the harpers in to "sing" of her husband's death, Yeats tells Irish men and women that they must "sing" of the great O'Rahilly's heroic end:

> Sing of the O'Rahilly,
> Do not deny his right;
> Sing a "the" before his name;
> Allow that he, despite
> All those learned historians,
> Established it for good;
> He wrote out that word himself,
> He christened himself with blood.
>
> (1–8)

Irish history, it would seem, is itself a funereal pageant of "terrible beauty," with a long procession of tragic actors:

> Come gather round me, players all
> come praise Nineteen-Sixteen
> Those from the pit and gallery
> Or from the painted scene
> That fought in the Post Office
> Or round the City Hall,
> Praise every man that came again,
> Praise every man that fell.
> From mountain to mountain ride the fierce horsemen.
>
> ("Three Songs to the One Burden," 55–63)

Yeats's use of the oxymoron, a "terrible beauty" in "Easter 1916" may have been inspired not only by the "real" drama of Irish history, but also by the more poetic portrayal of that drama in the Abbey Theatre. Pearse's play *An Rí* (The King), Raymond Porter suggests, is a likely source for that inspiration.[101] The play, a one-act "Morality," set in medieval Ireland and written in the literary idiom of the Irish heroic tales rather than "caint na ndaoine"[102] (language of the people), provocatively fuses together the drama of Calvary with that of Ireland's epic heroes. Yeats greatly admired the play and had it produced at the Abbey Theatre on 17 May 1913, along with Rabindranath Tagore's *The Post Office* (a strangely prophetic title). The play centers upon Giolla na Naomh, a type of boy Cuchulain-Christ figure who goes off to die for Ireland in answer to the "terrible, beautiful voice that comes out of the heart of battles."[103] The Abbot in the play connects this voice with heroic death: "The terrible, beautiful voice has spoken to this child. O herald death you shall be answered."[104] The oxymoronic phrase is repeated constantly throughout the play, and the following lines spoken by the Abbot to the young boys reflect that strange courtship with death we see throughout Irish history:

> Do you think if that terrible, beautiful voice for which young men strain their ears were to speak from yon place where the fighters are, and the horses, and the music, that I would stay you, did ye rise to obey it? Do you think I would grudge the dearest of these little boys, to death calling with that terrible, beautiful voice. . . ?[105]

An intoxication with death pervades the play. The following lines capture the intensity of that intoxication:

> FIRST MONK. That music of the fighters makes drunk the hearts of young men.
>
> SECOND MONK. It is good for young men to be made drunk.
>
> ABBOT. There is a heady ale which all young men should drink, for he who has not been made drunk with it has not lived. It is with that ale that God makes drunk the hearts of the saints. I would not forbid you your intoxication, O young men![106]

In a country where history has become poetry and poetry history, where reality and fantasy are often inextricably intertwined, Pearse's *An Ri*, a play which appears in every respect to be a dramatic rehearsal for the Easter Rising, would be a fitting source for Yeats's inspiration.

Another likely source for Yeats's phrase "a terrible beauty" is Joseph Sheridan Le Fanu's long poem *Duan na Glaev* (The Legend of the Glaeve).[107] Le Fanu writes of a beautiful Munster goddess named Fionula who is a priestess of mystery and death. Like Cathleen Ni Houlihan, she demands the ultimate sacrifice of her devotees, and Cathair, a young hero like Cuchulain, gladly accepts death for her sake. Although she has been dead many years, she still haunts the men of Ireland, luring them with her "terrible beauty":

> Fionula the Cruel, the brightest, the worst,
> With a terrible beauty the vision accurst,
> Gold-filleted, sandalled, of times dead and gone
> Far-looking, and harking, pursuing, goes on;
> Her white hand from her ear lifts her shadowy hair
> From the lamp of her eye floats the sheen of despair;
> Her cold lips are apart, and her teeth in her smile
> Glimmer death on her face with a horrible wile.[108]

Whatever the source, Yeats's phrase perfectly captures not only the tragic beauty of the Easter Rising, but the whole passionate tapestry of Ireland's troubled past and the marvelous poetry that has been woven from that tapestry.

Yeats, approaching his own death, does not alter the ancient form of that tapestry, but enriches its design. Like the poets of 1916, and the heroes that have gone before them, he responds to that "terrible, beautiful voice" of death with passion. In his poem "The Apparitions," written in April 1938, Yeats "speaks of death in sexual images and goes forth like Antony to meet darkness as a bride, with passion and befitting fear":[109]

> When a man grows old his joy
> Grows more deep day after day,
> His empty heart is full at length,
> But he has need of all that strength
> Because of the increasing Night
> That opens her mystery and fright.
>
> (17–22)

Yeats's philosophy of death was sensual and highly poetic, as the following letter written to Ethel Mannin on 9 October 1938, reveals:

> . . . a man's death is born with him and if his life is successful and he escapes mere mass death, his nature is completed by his final union with it. . . . In my own philosophy the sensuous image is changed from time to time at predestined moments called Initiationary Moments. . . . One sensuous image leads to another because they are never analyzed. At the critical moment they are dissolved by analysis and we enter by free will pure unified experience. When all the sensuous images are dissolved we meet true death. . . . This idea of death suggests to me Blake's design . . . of the soul and body embracing. All men with subjective natures move towards a possible ecstasy. . . .[110]

Yeats's belief that a man's death is born with him expresses the same idea as the Irish folk belief in the "sod of death," and the Old Irish poem which talks of death as "nut ripe falling to earth" reflects Yeats's belief that a man's nature is completed by his final union with death.

Richard Ellmann, commenting on Yeats's letter, notes that for Yeats the odyssey through life from birth to death is similar to the process of creating a poem. The landscape of a poem begins with a series of sensuous images which are dissolved at the critical moment by analysis. At that moment, image and idea are fused into a new whole which represents the completed poem.[111] If a man leads a fulfilling life, then his death can be an aesthetic experience similar to the completion of a beautiful poem. Yeats viewed his own death that way and, like a Celtic warrior poet, joyfully prepared for his participation in the ultimate heroic ritual:

> . . . I know for certain that my time will not be long. I have put away
> everything that can be put away that I may speak what I have to speak, and
> I find "expression" is a part of study. In two or three weeks . . . I will begin
> to write my most fundamental thoughts and the arrangement of thought
> which I am convinced will complete my studies. I am happy, and I think
> full of an energy, of an energy I had despaired of. It seems to me that I have
> found what I wanted. When I try to put all into a phrase I say, "Man can
> embody truth but he cannot know it." I must embody it in the completion
> of my life. . . .[112]

It is clear that, as Yeats moved towards the completion of his life, he was
experiencing the "ecstasy" he spoke of in his letter to Ethel Mannin. And
when the time came for him to die, he did not shrink from its unknown terror
but, like Cuchulain and the men of 1916, accepted its "terrible beauty" with
joy.

Even Yeats's place of burial can be seen as a highly symbolic poem, for in
death Yeats has placed himself in the very center of that great Irish matrix he
wrote about a year before he died. Surrounded by ancient burial chambers
and druidic ruins which dot the countryside around Drumcliff, Yeats's grave
stands in the center of a great Celtic spiral, with a round tower and a Celtic
cross nearby. Close by, Queen Maeve's burial mound stands majestically on
Knocknarea, and megalithic tombs cover the slopes of Ben Bulben. The
churchyard of St. Columba's Church, in which Yeats is buried, was built on
the site of an ancient monastery founded by St. Columba, which in turn
stands on the site of a more ancient Druid school. Yeats is careful to remind
us in "Under Ben Bulben" that no ordinary cross stands by his grave but an
"ancient" Celtic one. The Celtic Cross is a masterpiece of spiritual passion,
carved in delicate interlacing spirals and exact geometric designs. Each
separate spiral on the cross winds its way into the next, so that the huge
surface of the cross represents a magnificent intertwining of strange and
mysterious forms which seem to be reaching higher and higher as if to
connect with some more subtle and infinite beauty beyond the world. The
Celtic Cross is a perfect symbol for a poet like Yeats who strove so hard to
achieve that intricate beauty, both in his life and in his art.

The Celtic Cross is also a perfect symbol for the Celtic imagination, for
"compared to the classical imagination, the Celtic imagination is indeed the
'infinite' compared to the 'finite.' "[113] In its search for an elusive beauty, the
Celtic imagination has often "worn itself out in mistaking dreams for real-
ities."[114] In the preface to *Cuchulain of Muirthemne*, Yeats captures the
quality of this imagination:

> We think of actual life when we read those Norse stories, . . . but the Irish
> stories make us understand why the Greeks call myths the activities of the
> daemons. The great virtues, the great joys, the great privations come in
> myths, and, as it were, take mankind between their naked arms, and

without putting off their divinity. Poets have taken their themes more often from stories that are all, or half, mythological, than from history or stories that give one the sensation of history, understanding, as I think, that the imagination which remembers the proportions of life is but a long wooing, and that it has to forget them before it becomes the torch and the marriage-bed.[115]

Reality does not long remain unchanged once it has entered the realm of the Irish imagination, for Irish "imaginativeness and melancholy are alike a passionate, turbulent, indomitable reaction against the despotism of fact."[116] Death, being the ultimate "fact" and the harshest reality, presents the greatest challenge to the Irish imagination and ultimately, through that imagination, becomes the greatest poetry. We shall be a long time forgetting the beautiful sentences uttered by Emer over the body of Cuchulain in Lady Gregory's *Cuchulain of Muirthemne:*

"And oh! my love!" she said, we were often in one another's company, and it was happy for us, for if the world had been searched from the rising of the sun to sunset, the like would never have been found in one place, of the Black Sainglain and the Grey of Macha, and Laege the chariot-driver, and myself and Cuchulain. And after that Emer bade Conall to make a wide, very deep grave for Cuchulain; and she laid herself down beside her gentle comrade, and she put her mouth to his mouth, and she said: "Love of my life, my friend, my sweetheart, my one choice of the men of the earth, many is the woman, wed or unwed, envied me until today; and now I will not stay living after you."[117]

From the anonymous author of the tenth-century poem on destiny who talks of death as "nut-ripe falling to the earth" to Seamus Heaney who looks at a modern Irish funeral and longs for "ceremony" and ancient "rhythms," we see the desire to turn all to beauty, to turn all to art—this is the imaginative legacy of Yeats's Irish tapestry. It is remarkable that in April 1916, while Pearse was preparing to turn his own death and Irish history into art, Yeats had just completed an essay in which he ponders the connection between death and art: "I believe that the elaborate technique of the arts, seeming to create out of itself a superhuman life, has taught more men to die than oratory or the Prayer Book."[118] This is certainly true of art in Ireland, where the Irish Literary Movement, with Yeats as its high priest, made the old gods and heroes so attractive that a whole generation of young men flocked to imitate them: "Did that play of mine send out / Certain men the English shot?" Commenting on the hypnotic power of the poetic emblem or image over those about to die, Yeats writes:

The Minoan soldier who bore upon his arm the shield ornamented with the dove in the Museum at Crete, or had upon his head the helmet with the winged horse, knew his role in life. When Nobuzane painted the child

Saint Kobo Daishi kneeling full of sweet austerity upon the flower of the lotus, he set up before our eyes exquisite life and the acceptance of death.[119]

In that moment of incandescent passion which was the Easter Rising, Pearse and his fellow soldiers may not have had helmets with winged horses or shields with white doves, but they too turned to Mask and Image for their inspiration. They, too, turned all to art:

. . . in the imagination of Pearse and his fellow soldiers the Sacrifice of the Mass had found the Red Branch in the tapestry; they went out to die calling upon Cuchulain.

2

The Search for Beauty: Mask and Image in the Rising

"Put off that mask of burning gold
With emerald eyes."
"O no, my dear, you make so bold
To find if hearts be wild and wise,
And yet not cold."

"I would but find what's there to find,
Love or deceit."
"It was the mask engaged your mind,
And after set your heart to beat,
Not what's behind."

Yeats, "The Mask"

i

THE fierce beauty of Ireland's various feminine Masks, fashioned by her admirers through the centuries, "engaged" the minds of both Yeats and the 1916 poets and set their hearts to beat: "And what if excess of love / Bewildered them till they died" (72–73). "The Rose," "Cathleen Ni Houlihan," and many other feminine Masks proved irresistible to Irish poets because, according to Yeats, they were carved in the shadow of "ancient Queens" and bore the imprint of old legends:

Our mythology, our legends, differ from those of other European countries because down to the end of the seventeenth century they had the attention, perhaps the unquestioned belief, of peasant and noble alike; Homer belongs to sedentary men, even today our ancient Queens, our mediaeval soldiers and lovers, can make a pedlar shudder . . . we Irish poets, modern men also, reject every folk art that does not go back to Olympus.[1]

An examination of Irish art and archeology reveals that the fascination with Mask that we see in Yeats, in Wilde, and in the 1916 poets also "goes back" to

47

the great tapestry. The Mask, in both its plastic and symbolic forms, is rooted deep in the Celtic past. Ann Ross, in *Everyday Life of the Pagan Celts*, writes that "stylized human Masks" were a prominent motif in Celtic art and that in Ireland the fascination with such Masks continued "to an almost bewildering degree"[2] right through the Middle Ages. Macalister, in *The Archeology of Ireland*, points out that as late as the twelfth century, when the people of Clonfert wanted to build a church in honor of "the Lord Mighty in Battle,"[3] ancient pagan traditions were so strong that they did not consider it inappropriate to adorn the doorway of the Church with Masks—the strange reminders of a pagan past. And as Nora Chadwick, in *The Celts*, observes, even in Ireland today, mysterious stone Masks can be seen over the arches of many old churches, including the west doorway at Killeshin in County Laois and the doorway of St. Brendan's Cathedral in Galway.[4] Significantly, Yeats's poem, "The Double Vision of Michael Robartes," which is structured around the gyres and lunar cycles connected with the Mask, is set on the actual site of one of these old churches—Cormac's Chapel at Cashel. Cormac's Chapel is noted for the bizarre Masks that adorn its doorway. It is, therefore, a peculiarly appropriate site for the strange visions of Michael Robartes: "On the grey rock of Cashel the mind's eye / Has called up the cold spirits that are born / When the old moon is vanished from the sky / And the new still hides her horn" (1–4). The landscape of the poem, with its ecclesiastical ruins and strange pagan beasts—"A Sphinx with woman breast and lion paw," reflects a mysterious blend of pagan and Christian art. The poem, like many of Yeats's poems, is richly illuminated by the Druid-Christian tapestry that hangs behind it. Cashel was the renowned seat of the North Munster kings, both pagan and Christian. Its outstanding feature is the magnificent lofty rock which overlooks the surrounding land-scape. Before the coming of Christianity to Ireland, Corc, the pagan king of Munster, built a powerful stronghold on the summit of the rock, which then became the chief residence of the Munster kings and continued so until the twelfth century. In 1101 King Murketagh O'Brien handed it over to the ecclesiastical authorities and many splendid buildings were then built which remain today, among them Cormac's Chapel with its strange stone Masks. The very architecture of Cormac's Chapel with its bizarre animal figures and sinister Masks represents the perfect intertwining of Druid and Christian forms that Yeats admired so much. It symbolizes in ancient stone the "Unity of Culture defined and evoked by Unity of Image"[5] that Yeats desired for Ireland. The "double" vision of Michael Robartes, therefore, suggests much more than the fusion of life and death, of flesh and spirit, of chaos and art. It suggests the fusion of two cultures, one Christian and one pagan:

> The commonness of thoughts and images
> That have the frenzy of our western seas.

> Thereon I made my moan,
> And after kissed a stone,
>
> And after that arranged it in a song
> Seeing that I, ignorant for so long,
> Had been rewarded thus
> In Cormac's ruined house.
>
> (61–64)

Many of the Celtic Masks discovered in Ireland were Janus-faced (two faces on the same base, facing in opposite directions), and Ross sees this as perhaps a reflection of the power of the Celtic God to "look forward into the Otherworld and backwards into the world of mankind."[6] If this is so, then the Janus-faced Mask is a perfect symbol in "actual" form for Yeats's theory of the Antithetical Mask, for, according to Yeats's theory, the individual who dons the Antithetical Mask of the "Otherworld" still looks back into the empirical "world of mankind." The Mask is the form that holds both of these worlds in creative tension. As Gale Schricker, in her discussion of Yeats's Mask, points out, "the mask is only one part of a dynamic relationship," and it is the "dynamic poetic interplay" between the "transcendent and empirical aspects of the one self . . . that explores and reveals the potentials and limitations of the compound self."[7] Gerhard Herm, in his book on the Celts, notes that the Janus-form Masks discovered by archeologists are historical evidence that the Celts were fond of depicting their gods as "dual" beings.[8] A fascinating example of this duality can be seen in the strange metamorphic personality of Cuchulain in the *Tain*. Cuchulain at times becomes so "transformed utterly" that he does, indeed, appear to take on a second personality, and this second personality is so diametrically opposed to his "daily self" that it constitutes what Yeats would describe as an Antithetical Mask. This dramatic transformation, which is physical as well as psychological, occurs at those moments when Cuchulain is seized by battle rage. The following passage from Lady Gregory's *Cuchulain of Muirthemne*, describes this transformation:

> He went out then against the men of Ireland, and attacked them, and his anger came on him, so that it was not his own appearance he had on him, but the appearance of a god. . . . But the next day he was standing on the hill, young, and comely, and shining, and the cloud of his anger was gone from him. . . . And there was wonder on these women to see him so quiet and so gentle today, and he such a terror to the whole army yesterday.[9]

Lady Gregory, however, omits the detailed descriptions of Cuchulain's transformation that we find in the original saga because she found them too grotesque. For explicit descriptions of Cuchulain's metamorphosis, we must turn to Thomas Kinsella's translation of the *Tain:*

The first warp-spasm swized Cuchulain. . . . On his head the temple-sinews stretched to the nape of his neck, each mighty, immense, measureless knob as big as the head of a month-old child. He sucked one eye so deep into his cheek out of the depths of his skull; the other eye fell out along his cheek. His mouth weirdly distorted. . . . The hair of his head twisted like the tangle of a red thornbush stuck in a gap. . . .[10]

It is amazing that these grim distortions can be found in "actual" form in real Celtic Masks. Archeologists discovered Celtic Masks with distorted features—the small eye on one side of the head and the huge eye on the other, the twisted mouth, the bizarre hair, and so on, which N.E. Sanders notes are all suggestive of Cuchulain when his distortions are upon him.[11] Thus, Cuchulain, the symbol of a modern rising that excelled in the manipulation of Mask, appears also to have been a popular subject for these ancient Mask makers who expressed in their strange Masks the "terrible beauty" of the legends and myths that surrounded them. Masks play an interesting part in those legends and sagas, for Yeats's "Catheads," which appear in *The Green Helmet*, find their prototypes in the Catheads depicted in *The Battle of Ventry*. And, as Macalister notes, these Catheads are really the magicians in their "zoomorphic dance-masks."[12]

Why did the Celtic fascination with Masks continue in Ireland "to an almost bewildering degree" to such a late date? And why did Yeats and the 1916 poets return to the concept of Mask as a vehicle for poetic and nationalistic expression? Perhaps we can find some clues to this mystery in Irish art. George Sigerson writes that the ancient Gaels "polished, shaped, and set their poetry, not as word-smiths, but as word-jewelers, dealing with gems."[13] This quality made them outstanding craftsman, and examples of their artistic skill can be seen in the exquisite effects they produced in their illuminated manuscripts, in their works in gold and silver, and above all in their poetry, which, at its best, had the beauty of a cut diamond.[14] Aodh de Blacam notes that the Irish past cannot be understood by men who forget that, amid so much that was chaotic, craftsman and scribes sought ever finer delicacies, and "scholastic poets won ever more elaborate harmonies from language."[15] Gaelic poetry, de Blacam writes, reaches a luxuriance of assonance and alliteration (both in its scholastic and late popular forms) unknown in other languages, and every stressed syllable must satisfy a strict metrical pattern.[16] Form, however, was not stressed at the sacrifice of content, and it has been said that Irish is "the language for your prayers, your curses, and your love-making,"[17] for it is unusually rich in terms expressive of the emotions, and its expressiveness is strengthened by its rhythm of form and fullness of sound.[18] These qualities, de Blacam points out, no doubt spring from that intensity which is typically Celtic. He notes that the Celt is famous for his love of superlatives and the denationalized Celt, deprived of the restraints of his native culture, becomes blatant. The Gaelic language, however, controls this tendency towards exaggeration and excessive emotion, and the perfection of style that is demanded "curbs the turbulence of matter."[19] Passion is there but is channeled into finely formed phrases. "Gaelic poetry, therefore, finds its beauty in restrained energy, like that of a wild creature straining at the leash"[20] or, as Yeats puts it, "beauty like a tightened bow."[21]

Is not Yeats aiming for just this effect in his own poetry when he declares in "The Fisherman" that "Before I am old / I shall have written him one / Poem maybe as cold / And passionate as the dawn" (37–40)? And is not the Mask, in both its symbolic and plastic form, a vehicle, like Gaelic poetry, which channels energy into form without sacrificing either? Certainly the Mask in its plastic form is one of the most precisely "carved" of objects, yet its exact geometry works like the precise form of Gaelic poetry, to suggest "restrained" energy rather than the "lack" of energy. In his essay on the Noh plays, Yeats speaks of the dynamic rigidity of the Mask:

> A Mask will enable me to substitute for the face of some commonplace player . . . the fine invention of a sculptor . . . nor shall we lose by stilling the movement of the features. . . . Who can forget the face of Chaliapine as the Mogul King in Prince Igor when a Mask covering its upper portion made him seem like a phoenix at the end of its thousand wise years awaiting in condescension the burning nest, and what did it not gain from that immobility in dignity and power?[22]

As we shall see in Chapter 3, Yeats achieved much of this "dignity and power" in his creation of Fand's Mask in *The Only Jealousy of Emer* (a play where the players wore real Masks). Fand, who is obviously a personification of Ireland herself in but another of her hypnotic Masks, wears a beautiful gold Mask that is truly "the fine invention of a sculptor"—a Mask that is as "cold and passionate as the dawn."

From the ancient Celts and their Janus-faced Masks to modern Irish poets like Yeats, the concept of Mask has been an integral part of the poetic landscape of Ireland. Yeats himself tells us that his ideas about the Mask are firmly rooted in the great Irish tapestry. In his autobiography he writes that his idea of the Mask was based on the numerous stories of changelings he and Lady Gregory had heard throughout the Irish countryside. According to Irish fairylore, the Sidhe sometimes kidnap a human individual and leave a Masklike image (a changeling) in his place. This ancient belief, Yeats tells us, inspired his "Doctrine of the Mask":

> Lady Gregory and I heard many tales of changelings, grown men and women as well as children, who as the people believe are taken by the fairies, some spirit remaining in their stead, and I constantly asked myself what reality there could be in these tales, often supported by so much testimony. I awoke one night to find myself lying upon my back with all my limbs rigid, and to hear a cermonial measured voice which did not seem to

be mine, speaking through my lips, "We make an image of him who sleeps," it said, "and it is not him who sleeps, and we call it Emmanuel." After many years that thought, others often found as strangely being added to it, became the thought of the Mask, which I have used in these memoirs to explain men's characters.[23]

Yeats's Cuchulain play, *The Only Jealousy of Emer,* where all the players wear Masks, revolves around the changeling tradition. In the play, Emer and Eithne Inguba speak of the "image" that has been put by the Sidhe in Cuchulain's place and talk of driving the changeling out:

EMER: It may be
          An image has been put in his place.
          A sea-borne log bewitched into his likeness,
          Or some stark horsemen grown too old to ride
          Among the troops of Manannan, Son of the Sea,
          Now that his joints are stiff.

EITHNE: Cry out his name. All that are taken from
          sight, they say,
          Loiter amid the scenery of their lives
          For certain hours or days, and should he hear
          He might, being angry, drive the changeling out.[24]

Yeats's idea of the Mask was, of course, not a static concept but a constantly evolving one and during the course of its evolution was strongly influenced by Wilde, Dowden, Blake, Blavatsky, and others. Nevertheless, Yeats himself tells us that his first idea of the Mask came about as a result of his thoughts about the changeling tradition in Irish fairylore—a belief still prevalent in rural Ireland. Furthermore, in his essay in *Lucifer* on fairy dynasties, Yeats points out that the fairies are descendants of the Tuatha de Danaan[25]—that ancient mystical race whose magicians and artists excelled in Maskmaking. Thus, from ancient Ireland to modern Ireland, the Mask has played an important part in the history of the Irish imagination, and the fascination with Mask exhibited by both Yeats and the 1916 poets seems to confirm, in a remarkable way, Yeats's belief in the existence of an unbroken psychic link connecting the two Irelands together.

Given Yeats's belief in the evocative power of the Mask, it is not surprising that he should turn to the Mask as a means of revitalizing national feeling. Six years before the Easter Rising, Yeats, complaining that national feeling was dying out and stressing Ireland's need for a Mask and Image to sustain her, wrote in his diary:

You cannot keep the idea of a nation alive . . . without a model of it in the mind of the people. . . . You must have a complex mass of images, something like an architect's model. The Young Ireland poets created a mass of images that filled the minds of the young . . . and entered so into the affections that they followed men on to the scaffold. . . . Our movement thought to do the same thing in a more profound and therefore more enduring way.[26]

Over the years, Yeats, in his poetry, plays, and prose, had been busy assembling that "complex mass of images" from Irish mythology and Irish history. By 1916, the Mask he had forged of Ireland was so powerful that Oliver St. John Gogarty, standing in the Irish Senate some years later, declared that, without Yeats's vision of Ireland in 1916, there would have been no Free State.[27] Pearse shared Gogarty's exalted view of Yeats's role as Maskmaker in the birth of the Irish Republic, for, in the June 1913 issue of *Irish Freedom*, Pearse hailed Yeats as "the poet who has most finely voiced Irish nationalism in our time."[28]

Mask and Image were so crucial to the spiritual success of the Rebellion and were carved so carefully by Yeats and the 1916 poets in the years that preceded the Rebellion that the Rising itself seems but the natural unfolding of a great play that had its origins in the dramatic Images and Masks of Irish literature and drama. Pearse's vision of his own destiny and that of Ireland had been shaped by the romantic images of Gaelic literature and myth, and Yeats's portrayal of Cuchulain in *The Green Helmet* as the embodiment of those romantic ideals had deepened Pearse's appreciation of the great Irish hero.[29] Yeats had observed in "A General Introduction for my Work" that "Gaelic is incapable of abstraction,"[30] and he knew that the Irish hatred of abstraction extended into the area of politics, for traditionally so little was the abstract State admired that the very word *Stat* in Keating is a symbol for something alien and oppressive.[31] Yeats, therefore, set out to create a Mask for Ireland that would be as powerful as the image of Ireland found in the ancient sagas. Through his masterful use of Gaelic iconography, Yeats created for Pearse and his fellow soldiers that "architect's model" without which, he maintained, the "idea" of a nation cannot exist. When Pearse, therefore, wanted to engender feelings of patriotism in young Irish men and women, he did not use modern political slogans but filled his speeches with the powerful images of Yeats's great model:

> Fearghus, Conchubar, Cuchulain, Fion, Oisin . . . though well-nigh two thousand years have rolled away since those mighty heroes trod this land of ours, yet is their spirit not dead: it lives on in our poetry, in our music, in our language, and, above all, in the longings which we feel for a something, we know not what,—our irresistible, overmastering conviction that we, as a nation are made for higher things. . . .[32]

The emphasis that Pearse places on the Irish longing for some indefinable beauty, "for something, we know not what," echoes Yeats's description of the Irish imagination in the preface to *Cuchulain of Muirthemne* as one which is "always athirst for an emotion, a beauty which cannot be found in its perfection upon earth, or only for a moment." It is the relentless search for that beauty and the willingness to sacrifice all for the attainment of such beauty that connects the poet warriors of ancient Ireland with those of 1916. "Nationality," Pearse had written in "Ghosts," is a "spiritual" not a "material" thing. It is "a thing of beauty, a Jewel to be preserved at all peril."[33] Pearse's perception of nationality spans the centuries, for in Old and Middle Irish poetry liberty is represented not as something which will make men materially richer but as a "spiritual consummation."[34] The poets sing of the sweetness of life in Ireland, of the horrors of exile, and "of the union as between lovers, of the island and the race."[35]

The very identity of the Irish has always been tied up with their notion of beauty, and their notion of beauty inextricably tied up with their concept of nationality. That is why two of the most potent traditional icons of Irish nationality—the Rose and her masculine coun'erpart, Cuchulain, are both Masks that represent the perfect fusion of poetry, spirituality, and nationality. As mentioned earlier, Yeats has said that art "has taught more men to die than oratory or the Prayer Book." In Ireland, art itself has been that "Prayer Book," and it has not only taught men like Pearse and his comrades how to die, but also how to live. From its earliest origins, poetry in Ireland was invested with mystical significance and was in the hands of the priest poets—the Druids. As Yeats observes in "To Ireland in the Coming Times," Ireland has always been "a Druid land," singing "a Druid tune" (32). The Masks and Images created by these druids were sacred[36] and, as Aodh de Blacam notes, at all times the poet held a privileged position in Ireland: "Bishop, king and 'ard-ollamh,' or chief poet had equal dignity."[37] Old Irish writers, when referring to that ancient time when Ireland rose out of the void, cite with something akin to religious worship the mysterious, runic poem of the first poet of Ireland—the Milesian Druid poet Amergin. Amergin is the prototype of all those poet patriots down through the ages, who used a feminine Mask to personify Ireland. In the following lines Amergin refers to Ireland as "the great lady Ireland" and calls upon her to be fertile by receiving the fathers of the race—Eremon, Eber and Ir as lovers:

> Ailiu iath nErend.
> Ermach muir mothuch,
> mothach sliabh streathach,
> screathach coill ciothach
> ciothach ab essach
>
> (I invoke the land of Ireland.
> Much-coursed be the fertile sea,
> fertile be the fruit-strewn mountain,
> fruit-strewn be the showery wood). . . .

> be adbal Ere,
> Eremhon ortus,
> Ir, Ebir ailsius.
> Ailiu iath nErenn.
>
> (the great lady Ireland,
> Eremon hath conquered her,
> Ir, Eber have invoked for her.
> I invoke the land of Ireland).[38]

This fragment is believed to be 3,000 years old. The poem is highly significant for it shows that, from time immemorial, the creation of life itself, as well as the concept of nationality, has been mingled in the Irish imagination with poetic creation. Most importantly, it reflects the continuity of a tradition that portrays Ireland through a poetic Mask as a woman—a tradition that sees that woman as a mystical and national symbol and then speaks in highly sexual terms of the relationship between that woman and her poets. The sexual language Irish poets often used when addressing Ireland can be seen in Eochy O'Hussey's love poem to Ireland, written in 1589. O'Hussey tells Ireland: "Suirgheach sin a Eire ogh (This is love-making for you, O virgin Eire)."[39] We have seen numerous examples of this erotic language in the love-death poems of the 1916 poets, and, as we shall see in Chapter 3, Yeats's Cuchulain plays revolve around the "terrible beauty" of this tradition.

In order fully to understand the deep emotions such feminine Masks evoked in Irish patriots, especially the 1916 poets who went out to die with the image of the Black Rose in their hearts, one must realize that life for the Irish was so barren under British rule that often the Mask they had created of Ireland was all they had to sustain them. And when England set out to anglicize Ireland by the deliberate and systematic extermination of her ancient traditions, language, and culture, the Irish felt she was destroying their very souls. Generation after generation of Irish men and women were born with a burning hatred of English rule and with what Yeats describes as a "fanatic heart":

> Out of Ireland have we come
> Great hatred, little room,
> Maimed us at the start
> I carry from my mother's womb
> a fanatic heart.
>
> ("Remorse for Intemperate Speech," 11–15)

Out of this "great hatred" of English repression arose an even greater passion to preserve the ancient traditions and Masks of Ireland. A brief description of the heroic struggle of the Irish poet during the centuries of English rule will help us to understand the "excess of love" for Ireland that Yeats writes about in "Easter 1916" and the spiritual concept of nationality which the 1916 poets inherited from their ancestors and which propelled them towards making the ultimate sacrifice in 1916.

By the fourteenth century, the English were fully aware that the Irish bards were one of the principal bulwarks of Irish nationality. In order to silence them the English passed the Statute of Kilkenny in 1357, which forbade patronage of the bardic art and learning. This law initiated a lasting policy of hostility to the profession, and, with the coming of the Reformation in the sixteenth century, the situation in Ireland for Irish poets became bleak indeed. The extirpation of the Catholic faith in Ireland and the welding together of Ireland and England into one religious and political unit were the goals of the Tudor monarchs.[40] An unknown Irish poet bemoans the fate of Irish poets and nobles under Elizabeth: "A uaisle Innse Seanairt / neamhmaith mur gceim ar gclaochludh (O nobles of the Island of Art, evil is your change of dignity)."[41] The final horror of English rule in Ireland is reflected in the infamous Penal Laws which were enacted in the seventeenth century.[42] According to de Blacam, the seventeenth century was the most tragic and the most brilliant century in the history of Irish letters. In the literature of this age we see the painful transition from the aristocratic Gaelic order to the secret Ireland of the Penal days. The Penal Laws sentenced "the proudest and most ancient nation of Western Europe to a condition worse than Egyptian servitude."[43] English Penal law, in the words of one of its chief exponents, did not "presume such a person as an Irish Catholic to exist."[44] During the period of the Penal Laws, the whole native governing class either became outlaws, hiding out in the hills, or went into exile. Yeats praises the Irish for preserving their ancient heritage during this terrible time:

> The "Irishry" have preserved their ancient "deposit" through wars which, during the sixteenth and seventeenth centuries, became wars of extermination; no people, Lecky said at the opening of his *Ireland in the Eighteenth Century,* have undergone greater persecution, nor did that persecution altogether cease up to our own day. No people hate as we do in whom the past is always alive.[45]

Although the age was a tragic one for Ireland, it was not without a certain heroic beauty. De Blacam believes that there is no chapter in the literary history of Europe of deeper humane interest than that supplied by Penal Ireland; for here we find a people, ravaged by famine and disease, reduced to the most terrible poverty, nevertheless cherishing a copious poetry.[46] Scribes worked incessantly, multiplying copies of the ancient sagas and copying bardic and later poetry.[47] The life of these Irish was so centered in beauty that they simply could not tolerate life without it and were willing to face even death rather than turn away from their native art. As a result, they formed a clandestine institution called "Cuirt na h'Eigse" (The Court of Poetry),[48] which nourished the secretive literary life. In a barn, or other hidden place, men would assemble and recite the poems they had written as they worked in their conqueror's fields. Points of meter, vocabulary and history would be discussed and the members would pool their Gaelic lore. Thus was the purity of the language guarded and the ancient traditions of the great tapestry preserved. The Courts flourished as feasts of poetic delight and provided a spiritual escape from the age.[49] As we read the "Aislingi" or "vision" poems written during this age, we sense in this secret Ireland the formation of a poetic Mask whose lineaments reflect the mystical ideal beauty that Yeats describes in "The Secret Rose," as that "Far-off, most secret, and inviolate Rose":

> Far-off, most secret, and inviolate Rose,
> Enfold me in my hour of hours; where those
> Who sought thee in the Holy Sepulchre,
> Or in the wine-vat, dwell beyond the stir
> And tumult of defeated dreams; and deep
> Among pale eyelids, heavy with the sleep
> Men have named beauty. . . .
>
> (1–7)

Since it was dangerous for Irish poets during this time to mention the name of Ireland in their poetry, they were forced to retreat into poetic symbolism and to create a Mask that symbolized Ireland while pretending to refer to something else. Thus, what Irish poets had chosen to do previously for poetic reasons, they were now forced to do for political reasons. During this time, Irish poets wrote of Ireland as a maiden of extraordinary beauty who had been deprived of her lover.[50] And the poetic Mask of Ireland carved by the poets during these troubled years was the very antithesis of the actual denuded and violated Ireland of British occupation—hence its Antithetical Mask. This Mask, however, paradoxically "revealed" rather than "concealed" the true essence and beauty of the "hidden" Ireland, just as Yeats's Antithetical Mask reveals to the individual who embraces it his deepest if most "hidden" self. As lovers of Ireland, these poets were doing what all true lovers do, according to Yeats's theories of the Mask:

> It seems to me that true love is a discipline, and it needs so much wisdom that the love of Solomon and Sheba must have lasted, for all the silence of the Scriptures. Each divines the secret self of the other, and refusing to believe in the mere daily self, creates a mirror where the lover or the beloved sees an image to copy in daily life; for love also creates the Mask.[51]

These Irish poet-lovers created in their poetry, a "mirror" that bypassed Ireland's "daily self," and reflected only her "secret self." In so doing, they created the most exquisite Mask.

If the ancient Irish aristocratic order was broken into fragments by the

Battle of Kinsale,[52] the Statute of Kilkenny and the Penal Laws, the Courts
of Poetry went a long way towards piecing those fragments back together
again through the creation of such a powerful Mask. This Mask helped to
stem the "invulnerable tide" ("Cuchulain's Fight with the Sea," 87) of
English rule in Ireland—at least in the cultural sense. And Ireland, despite
its oppression, like the aged man in "Sailing to Byzantium," continued to
"clap its hands and sing, and louder sing / for every tatter in its mortal dress"
(11–12). The Courts of Poetry, proved, ultimately, that neither English law
nor English guns could kill the desire for beauty which was part of the Irish
soul.

The power this feminine Mask exerted over the minds of the Irish poets
and patriots down through the years can be seen in the intensity of their
anger towards England. Keating saw England's defilement of Ireland's
beauty as the epitome of evil and Keating's description of Ireland as "the
harlot of England"[53] was something Pearse never forgot. In "From a Hermitage," Pearse writes that the phrase used by Keating would, in modern
Ireland, "no longer be a terrible metaphor, but a more terrible truth . . . for
is not Ireland's body given up to the pleasure of another, and is not Ireland's
honour for sale in the market places?"[54] Yeats, looking at the barren "image"
Ireland had become under British rule, asks:

> Was it for this the wild geese spread
> The grey wing upon every tide;
> For this that all that blood was shed,
> For this Edward Fitzgerald died,
> And Robert Emmet and Wolfe Tone,
> All that delirium of the brave?
> Romantic Ireland's dead and gone
> It's with O'Leary in the grave.
>
> ("September 1913," 17–24)

Both Yeats and Pearse knew that only the "delirium of the brave," or the
radical courage of a Cuchulain, could restore the beauty of "Romantic
Ireland" and bring back to her tarnished Mask the burnished glory of a
greater day. And both men, as Irish poets who lived in a world of image and
symbol, knew the important role Mask and Image could play in arousing the
fervor of patriotism. Pearse stressed the importance of ancient patriotic
symbols in the creation of a new Ireland and praised the Catholic Church for
her artistic manipulation of image and symbol:

> The wise Church that has called into her service all the arts, knows better
> than any other institution, human or divine, the immense potency of
> symbols, with symbols she exorcises evil spirits, with symbols she calls
> into play for beneficent purposes the infinite powers of omnipotence. And

those of her children who honour not her symbols she pronounces anathema.[55]

Pearse also wrote in the same essay that "a gibbet has come to be the noblest symbol in the world, because it symbolises the noblest thing that has ever been done among men."[56]

Plunkett and MacDonagh were also fascinated by the "immense potency" of patriotic Masks and Images as a means of "exorcising" the "evil spirits" of England from Irish soil. MacDonagh's son Donagh writes that his father spent a great deal of time hunting through the pages of books for the "significant and memorable image"[57] with which to express some nationalistic ideal, and in his poem "Images" MacDonagh reveals his reverence for antique images: "The images of old / Reverently I hold / And here entemple, enstate."[58] Plunkett, too, was fascinated by the powerful "image," and the voice of Plunkett as it emerges in the symbolic landscape of his poetry is that of the Irish poet warrior who will use his "images" of light—his "blades and tongues of fire"[59]—as weapons against the English powers of darkness which were enveloping Ireland. As Osborn Bergin points out in *Bardic Poetry*, traditionally words have been used by the Irish as lethal weapons, and in ancient Ireland one of the most feared and revered members of society was the satirist. The satirist was looked upon as a kind of magician, a weaver of spells and incantations, who could destroy his enemies by the venom of his verse.[60] In the *Tain*, for example, Fergus describes the powers of the poet satirist Aithirne as being so great that "the rivers and the lakes went back before him when he made a satire on them, and rose when he praised them."[61] And when Queen Maeve saw that it was impossible to beat Cuchulain by physical force on the battlefield, she sent her satirist out to fight Cuchulain with words. When Buck Mulligan, in *Ulysses*, calls Stephen Dedalus "Kinch, the knife-blade"[62] because of the cutting quality of his speech, he too is expressing an idea that has its roots deep in Irish tradition. As Kenneth Hurlstone Jackson observes in *The Oldest Irish Tradition*, the fear of the satire of poets is still very much alive in rural Ireland.[63]

Language, then, in Ireland has been used both as a sacred instrument of beauty and a deadly weapon of awesome power. And always the poet sought the powerful "Image" or Mask to seduce his readers. Often, the poet was totally seduced by the Masks he himself had created. This was certainly true of Yeats, who admitted that at times "Players and painted stage took all my love / And not those things that they were emblems of" ("The Circus Animals' Desertion," 31–32). And it was also true of the 1916 poets who not only assumed in real life the heroic Masks of the "players" Yeats had fashioned, but also entered totally into the Masks they themselves had created. Yeats had prophetically written in "Hodos Chameliontos" that the potent "Image . . . may be an originating impulse to revolution or to philosophy

. . ."[64] and he believed that he and his fellow poets could "remake" Ireland if they could find the right Mask: "Our towns are copied fragments from our breast; / And all man's Babylons strive but to impart / The grandeurs of his Babylonian heart."[65] Yeats stressed again and again the hypnotic power of the potent image:

> From what but the image of Apollo, fixed always in memory and passion, did his priesthood get that occasional power of lifting great stones and snapping great branches; and did not Gemma Galbani . . . in 1889 cause deep wounds to appear in her body by contemplating her crucifix. . . ? I had heard . . . that citizens of ancient Egypt assumed, when in contemplation, the image of their gods.[66]

By contemplating the Masks and Images of the great Irish tapestry, the 1916 poets, like the priesthood of ancient Greece, became fused with extraordinary power. And on Easter Monday, they proceeded to snap the "great branches" of the British Empire. The Easter Rebellion proved dramatically that Yeats was right when he remarked that the powerful "Image may be an originating impulse to revolution. . . ." And it is uncanny how Yeats's aesthetic theories, particularly his "Doctrine of the Mask," were confirmed by the poetic quality of the Rebellion. Even Yeats's theories about the significant role moments of crisis play in leading individuals to the Mask were corroborated by the actions of the rebels. By entering so completely into the Images of their contemplation, the poets, according to Yeats's doctrine of the Mask, called up those personifying spirits that Yeats describes as "Gates and Gate-keepers, because through their dramatic power they bring our souls to crisis, to Mask and Image, caring not a straw whether we be Juliet going to her wedding, or Cleopatra to her death; for in their eyes nothing has weight but passion."[67] Yeats writes that these spirits planned Dante's banishment, took his Beatrice, and "thrust Villon into the arms of harlots, and sent him to gather cronies at the foot of the gallows that Dante and Villon might through passion become conjoined to their buried selves, turn all to Mask and Image. . . ."[68] The 1916 poets, joined through "passion" to their buried selves, embraced the Mask of Cuchulain so completely that they began to see themselves as warriors of the Red Branch Knights, and the battle of 1916 became the battle of the *Tain*. If Yeats's theories of the Mask seem somewhat bizarre, one only has to look at the prophetic words of Pearse just several weeks before the Easter Rising to realize how accurate Yeats was about the seductive power of the Mask:

> The *Tain* and the Fionn story will come again in mighty dramas. The voice of a people that has been dumb for centuries will be heard anew; and it will make such music as has not been heard since Greece spoke the morning song of the free people.[69]

Pearse was right; the drama of the *Tain* did come again to Ireland; and on Easter Monday, when Pearse and his men went out to fight the British Empire, they knew as Cuchulain knew when he faced the enormous armies of Queen Maeve that death was inevitable:

> Some had not thought of victory
> But had gone out to die
> That Ireland's mind be greater
> Her heart mount up on high;
> And yet who knows what's yet to come?
> For Patrick Pearse had said
> That in every generation
> Must Ireland's blood be shed.
> From mountain to mountain ride the fierce horsemen.
>   ("Three Songs to the One Burden," 73–81)

Through their adoption of the heroic Mask, the rebels, according to Yeats, now embody the spirit of Cuchulain, one of those "fierce horsemen" who rode across the landscape of Milesian Ireland. The poets were so caught up in their symbolic Masks that they actually carried with them into a "modern" Rebellion the ancient emblem of Cuchulain—the sword. Ruth Dudley Edwards writes that Plunkett, in particular, looked as if he was participating in some ancient drama. His hands glittering with ancient Celtic rings, he unsheathed his sword as the group advanced towards the General Post Office.[70]

In an untitled fragment, Yeats once wrote: "The bravest from the gods but ask: A house, a sword, a ship, a mask."[71] In the years before the Rising, the poets employed two of these items—the sword and the Mask—in their fight against England. They are fitting emblems of the Rising, for the sword and the Mask represent that powerful combination of blood and poetry that finally brought English rule in Ireland to an end. One can not even begin to understand the Rising without discussing the poetry out of which the Rising grew and the Masks and images which were an integral part of that poetry, since the Rising itself was a work of art. The Rising was not merely a military phenomenon but also an aesthetic one, for in 1916 the cult of beauty was inextricably bound up with the cult of rebellion, and the worship of beauty was synonymous with the worship of Ireland herself. Pearse, Plunkett, and MacDonagh had not succumbed to the indolent luxury of worshipping art for art's sake, but rather sought art for Ireland's sake. And they brought all the powers of their poetic craft to bear upon the creation of the Rising. The Rising, in a sense, was their aesthetic masterpiece, and the high priest from whom they had received a great deal of their inspiration was Yeats. The personal utterances, poems, and plays of the rebels suggest that the Rising was "aesthetically" conceived by its poet leaders, and those writings that contain specific references to the Mask will be discussed later in this chapter. Although William Irwin Thompson brilliantly analyzes the Rebellion as a work of art and acknowledges the influence of Cuchulain and the Irish past on the rebels, he sees the real motives for their rebelling as personal. As a result, Thompson moves the discussion of the motivating factors behind the rebel's actions from the arena of Irish poetry and nationalism to the arena of Freudian psychology. This is where his argument becomes blurred. Thompson's failure to place the actions of the rebels in their proper historical, cultural, and poetic context leaves one with the false impression that Pearse and his comrades were no more than petulant adolescents who used the Rebellion as a means of narcissistic self-expression. Thompson decides that "artistically, the rebels were failures" and that because of this they gave themselves passionately to the Rebellion:

> The rebels of 1916 were something like the rebels of the student New Left today. Impatient with the philosophical, the ambiguous, the tragic, and the complex, they demand that issues be approached at gut level. . . . Artistically, the rebels were failures, and their failure could only intensify their yearnings for revolutionary satisfaction. . . . Failing in life the incompetent discovers that socially successful people are terrified by death and that he can finally become a success if he dies will. [72]

Referring again and again to Freud and to the pattern of "failed universe and return to humanity"[73] that he believes informs the actions of the poets, Thompson reduces the intense passions that lie behind Irish nationalism to a neat set of Freudian theories. At times this Freudian analysis takes on bizarre overtones. At one point Thompson suggests that MacDonagh's death "may well have been a gesture of despair at his countrymen who were not living up to the expectations he had of them."[74] It should be pointed out that MacDonagh was hardly the type of man who would risk death before a firing squad merely because he was disappointed with the Gaelic League. And although MacDonagh may not have been a great poet, to call him an artistic failure and label him an "incompetent" living in a "failed universe" is going too far. Yeats, for one, would not have approved of Thompson's Freudian analysis of MacDonagh's patriotism or his harsh judgment of MacDonagh's talent. Yeats admired MacDonagh's passionate intensity and felt he showed great artistic promise: "This other his helper and friend / Was coming into his force; / He might have won fame in the end" (26–28). Nor would Yeats have agreed with Thompson's view that Pearse was an artistic failure. Many of Pearse's poems and plays were well received in literary circles, and in a joint lecture which he and Pearse gave to the Trinity College Gaelic Society in November 1914, Yeats praised Pearse for his service to Irish literature.[75] In addition to writing poetry, plays, and short stories in both English and Irish, Pearse was actively involved in every aspect of Irish national life, and that life, by no stretch of the imagination, could be described as a failure. Pearse's writings, viewed through Thompson's Freudian lens, become dangerously distorted. Thompson, without indicating what specific works he is referring to, declares that Pearse's later writings exhibit "an almost pathological lust for violence":

> As Pearse moved into middle age, he became more desperate and violent. The tone of his earlier writings is meditative, lyrical, and human in his concern for education; but the tone of his later writing is not personal at all. . . . The imagery shows an almost pathological lust for violence. The desperation reveals just how much was at stake for Pearse psychologically, for if he slipped into old age without having taken arms, then his whole life, from his boyhood vow to the founding of his school, became meaningless and absurd. In the face of that threat, even action that failed would be a welcome relief from futility.[76]

In all fairness to Pearse, it should be pointed out that by nature he was anything but violent. He abhorred violence and turned to armed rebellion only as a last resort. All those who knew Pearse described him as a gentle, sensitive man who hated to see anyone or anything suffer—he once was so moved by a dead sparrow he found on his doorstep that he wrote a poem to it.[77] Raymond Porter notes that a terrible conflict raged within Pearse because of his decision to take militant action.[78] Pearse himself expresses his anguish about such action in the February 14 issue of *Irish Freedom:* "It is a terrible responsibility to be cast upon a man, that of bidding the cannon speak and the grapeshot pour."[79] Even at the height of the Rising when Pearse and his comrades occupied the General Post Office, Desmond Fitzgerald, the young poet who fought alongside Pearse, writes that Pearse was still haunted by that anguish. Fitzgerald reports that he and Pearse continually spoke of the moral rectitude of what they had done and Pearse brought in every theological argument and poetic quotation that justified the Rising.[80] This is hardly the behavior of a man who is "impatient with the philosophical, the ambiguous, the tragic, and the complex." Nor is it the behavior of a man who has "an almost pathological lust for violence." The "desperation" Thompson sees in Pearse's writings is not, as Thompson maintains, a desperation based on personal neurosis and the fear of growing old without taking arms. It is a "national" desperation experienced over and over again by Irish patriots who saw their country enslaved by England. The record of that desperation can be found in countless Irish poems stretching back to ancient Ireland. Many of these old Irish poems were translated by Pearse himself and his translations have been widely acclaimed. Pearse saw himself as part of a separatist tradition in Ireland that began with those patriots who fought against the Norman invaders in 1169.[81] Pearse's imagery and rhetoric must be examined within the context of that tradition if it is not to be misinterpreted, for, as Aodh de Blacam notes, the imagery employed by the Young Ireland poets and others like them finds its roots in the patriotic

Bardic poetry of the fourteenth century.[82] Thus, when Pearse praises young
Irish men for their willingness to "draw the sword of Ireland"[83] in order to
defend her honor and assert their virility, he is echoing the words of many
Irish poets before him. Sounding very much like Pearse, the fourteenth
century poet Geoffrey O'Dalaigh speaks of the relationship between Ireland
and her patriots in sexual terms: "Donal son of Donal shall capture brown-
eyed Eire, and joyously shall separate the Saxons from that grassy and long
pasturing plain."[84] The poet praises young Donal for his passionate love of
Ireland and for his willingness to forsake his "hobby horses of holly-rods for
colts of war-horses, fair rods for pointed spears and hurleys for swords."[85]
When Pearse, at the graveside of O'Donovan Rossa in 1915, declared that
"life springs from death; and from the graves of patriot men and women
spring living nations,"[86] he was not preaching some "new" radical gospel of
blood sacrifice, but reiterating a belief that pervades Irish history and
literature—a belief that is deeply imbedded in the racial imagination. Pearse's words are echoed in the title of a poem by Tadhg Camdhosach
O'Dalaigh written in 1380. The title, "Bean ar n-aitherigh Eire," translates as
"Eire is a woman newly arisen to life,"[87] and the poem expresses the belief
that, through the love and sacrifice of her poets and patriots (her lovers),
Ireland will experience a rebirth. Yeats's poem, "The Rose Tree," which
revolves around the blood sacrifice of Easter, focuses on this belief:

> "But where can we draw water,"
> Said Pearse to Connolly,
> "When all the wells are parched away?
> O plain as plain can be
> There's nothing but our own red blood
> Can make a right Rose Tree."
>
> ("The Rose Tree," 13–18)

It is important to remember that the 1916 poets were acting and writing in
a tradition that stretches back through the great tapestry to what Yeats
describes as some Irish "matrix out of which everything has come, some
condition that brought together as though into a single scheme 'exultations,
agonies and apparitions'. . . ."[88] The exultations, agonies and apparitions
Yeats speaks of have in Ireland, through the centuries, combined to create a
poetic-nationalistic tradition where sacrificial death for the Black Rose (as
discussed in Chapter 1) is celebrated. Thompson, however, fails to recognize
that the poets were acting strictly within this tradition, that their poems and
their actions reflect this tradition, and that they saw their death not as an
alternative to being successful poets but as an extension of the poetic and
heroic traditions they had inherited from ancient Ireland. Yeats puts it
perfectly in "The Galway Plains," where he writes of this tradition: "The man
who goest to death with the thought 'It was with the people I was' . . . has
behind him generations of poetry and poetical life."[89] And in the same essay

he wrote: "There is still in truth upon these great level plains a people, a community bound together by imaginative possession, by stories and poems which have grown out of its own life, and by a past of great passions which can still waken the heart to imaginative action."[90] Ireland, Yeats has written, "is a nation with ancient courage, unblackened fields, and a barbarous gift of self-sacrifice."[91]

J. Markale, in *Celtic Civilization*, points out that, while the act of sacrifice occupies an important position in every religion, our modern conception of the word is a modification of its original meaning, which has gradually altered over the centuries. Since the concept of sacrifice held by Pearse and his fellow poets in 1916 was, however, more in keeping with its ancient meaning as exemplified by Cuchulain, an examination of the origins of the word will shed some light on the almost voluptuous surrender to death we see in the leaders of the Rebellion. The word *sacrifice* actually derives from *sacrum facere*, which means *to make sacred*, and was used in ancient times to describe any act of self-transcending through which the individual sought to attain the divine.[92] Markale points out that Christianity has devalued the word by connecting it with ideas of austerity and self-denial. He adds that to regard sacrifice as a synonym for mortification is a serious error, since it totally alters the nature of that spiritual process by which the Ancients sought to fulfill their destiny. Ritual sacrifice, he notes, was never intended to deprive creation for the sake of the creator, but was a psychic procedure in which the sacrificial "victim" rose through a series of stages in his attempt to reach the divinity. Markale sees this form of sacrifice in the traditional alchemy practiced by men like Nicholas Flamel, Raymond Lulle or Basile Valentin. The quest for gold by way of the Philosopher's Stone is only the material cover for the real *oeuvre*, the metamorphosis of the individual.[93] In 1916, the "sacrificial" Mask of Cuchulain, was, like the Philosopher's Stone, an emblem through which the "metamorphosis of the individual" and the nation could be achieved. Yeats refers to this metamorphosis in his poem "The Statues," when he suggests that Pearse has been psychically transformed into Cuchulain: "When Pearse summoned Cuchulain to his side / What stalked through the Post Office?" (25–26), and again in his play *The Death of Cuchulain*, when he asks, "What stood in the Post Office? with Pearse and Connolly / Who thought Cuchulain till it seemed / He stood where they had stood?"[94]

Yeats's understanding of the term "self-sacrifice" is close to its ancient meaning, and his perception of it as a means towards spiritual illumination was shared by Pearse and the other executed poets. In "Estrangement," Yeats writes of a conversation in which he informs a friend that self-sacrifice and self-realization are not incompatible:

We discussed self-realization and self-sacrifice. He said that classic self-realization had failed and yet the victory of Christian self-sacrifice had plunged the world into the Dark Ages. I reminded him of some Norse God, who was hung over an abyss for three days, 'a sacrifice to himself' to show that the two were not incompatible.[95]

Yeats also draws an analogy between the idea of self-sacrifice and the creation of poetry, and he sees Synge's poetry as the result of a heroic struggle with his Antithetical Mask:

> I think that all noble things are the result of warfare, the division of a mind within itself, a victory, the sacrifice of a man to himself. I am certain that my friend's noble art, so full of passion and heroic beauty, is the victory of a man who in poverty and sickness created from the delight of expression, and in the contemplation that is born of the minute and delicate arrangement of images, happiness and health of mind.[96]

In "Dramatis Personae," Yeats writes: "Synge was a sick man picturing energy, a doomed man picturing gaiety."[97] Just as Synge's passionate poetry is the antithesis of his life and represents a victory over his ill health, the prophetic death poems of the rebels, written in such euphoric tones, reflect a victory over the terror of the deaths they must face. They show that Yeats was right when he said that self-sacrifice and self-fulfillment are not incompatible, and these poems, far from being the gestures of despair that Thompson has suggested, read like lyrical epiphanies of their approaching deaths. Pearse, for example, was so intoxicated with death that he wrote a "rann" to death. The word *rann* in Gaelic means *poem:*

> A rann I made within my heart
> To the rider, to the high King,
> A rann I made to my love,
> To the king of kings, ancient death.[98]

And MacDonagh in his poem, "O Star of Death," celebrates death as something opulent and beautiful:

> O star of death! I follow, till thou take
> My days to cast them from thee flake on flake,
> My rose of life to scatter bloom on bloom,
> Yet hold its essence in the phial rare
> Of life that lives with fire and air,
> With air that knows no dark, with fire not to consume.[99]

In another poem, MacDonagh sees death as the poetic completion of life—an attitude that is similar to that found in Irish folklore and in Yeats's philosophy of death:

> The Poet guards the philosophic soul
> In contemplation that no importunate thought

> May mar his ecstasy or change his song;
> And though he see the gloom and sing of sorrow,
> He is the world's Herald of Joy at last:
> His song is Joy, the music that needs sorrow
> To fill its closes, as Death fulfils Life,
> As Life fills Time, and Time Eternity:
> Joy that sees Death, yet in Death sees not woe.[100]

Plunkett, too, writes of this odyssey towards death with joy:

> Because I know the spark
> of God has no eclipse
> Now Death and I embark
> With laughter on our lips.[101]

Like Cuchulain in Yeats's play *The Death of Cuchulain*, who declares of his throat as it is about to be cut, "I say it is about to sing,"[102] Plunkett "laughs into the face of death."[103] And in his poem "The Splendour of God," Plunkett, in anticipation of the sacrificial metamorphosis and attainment of divinity that Markale describes, writes: "A brawling cataract is my blood / Of molten metal and fire—like God am I."[104]

The following words written about Seanchan in *The King's Threshold* could have been written about any of the executed leaders, so great was their ecstasy: "King, he is dead, some strange triumphant thought so filled his heart with joy that it has burst, being grown too mighty for your frailty."[105] In his *Autobiography*, Yeats defines this type of ecstasy as beauty: ". . . is not ecstasy some fulfillment of the soul in itself, some slow or sudden expansion of it like an overflowing well? Is not this what is meant by beauty?"[106]

Yukio Mishima, the Japanese novelist who committed hara-kiri on 25 November 1970 and who admits in *Sun and Steel* that he was influenced by Yeats,[107] also sees the ecstasy associated with heroic death as a form of beauty. In his book, he writes that the profoundest depths of the imagination lie in death. He states that the difference between a decadent and a heroic death resolves itself into the presence or absence of the idea of honor, which regards death as "something to be seen," and the presence or absence of the formal aesthetic of death that goes with it—in other words, the tragic nature of the approach to death and "the beauty of the body going to its doom."[108] Mishima bemoans the fact that modern man is almost devoid of the desire of the ancient Greeks to live "beautifully" and to die "beautifully," but he sees in the kamikaze suicide squad a return to the noble values of the Samurai, just as Yeats saw in the deaths of the rebel poets a return to the noble values of Cuchulain. Mishima states that man is often associated with beauty only through a heroic, violent death, since in ordinary life society maintains a careful surveillance to ensure that men shall have no part in beauty and that physical beauty in the male, when considered an "object" in itself without any intermediate agent, is despised. Mishima writes that society imposes a strict rule as far as men are concerned. It is this: "A man under normal circumstance must never permit his own objectivization; he can be objectified only through the supreme action—which is the moment of death,"[109] the moment when, even without being seen, the fiction of being seen and the beauty of the object are permitted. This "is the beauty of the suicide squad, which is recognized as beauty not only in the spiritual sense but, by men in general, in an ultra-erotic sense also."[110]

The Irish, like the Japanese, perceive in heroic death a beauty that is erotic as well as spiritual. In Ireland, Yeats writes, "the emotion that in other countries had made many love-songs has here been given, in a long wooing, to danger, that ghostly bride."[111] We are reminded here of Heaney's description of Ireland as an insatiable bride who swallows up her willing victims, and of the erotic poetry of death written by the 1916 poets. Pearse, like Mishima, saw the heroic shedding of blood as a sign of male virility. In "The Coming Revolution," he writes that "bloodshed is a cleansing and a sanctifying thing, and the nation which regards it as the final horror has lost its manhood."[112] As mentioned previously, the connection of virility with the shedding of blood finds its roots in Irish tradition. In *Cuchulain of Muirthemne*, Emer describes Cuchulain's virile beauty as being rich and sensual like "clear red blood,"[113] and her description of his body, which is covered with the wounds and scars of the potent warrior, is highly erotic:

> There is blood on his spear,
> There is blood on his sword,
> his white body is black with blood,
> his soft skin is furrowed with sword cuts.
> There are many wounds on his thighs.[114]

In the *Tain*, when the battle fury is upon Cuchulain and the "hero-halo" shines forth from his head, a "tall, thick, steady and strong . . . straight spout of black blood rises darkly and magically from the centre of his skull."[115]

Just a few weeks before the Easter Rebellion, Yeats published "The Noble Plays of Japan", in which he discussed the cult of art and blood practiced by the aristocratic warriors of medieval Japan. These warriors, like Cuchulain, exulted in poetry as well as blood:

> These soldiers, whose natures had as much of Walter Pater as of Achilles, combined with Buddhist priests and women to elaborate life in a ceremony, the playing of football, the drinking of tea, and all great events of State, becoming a ritual. In the painting that decorated their walls and in the poetry they recited one discovers the only sign of a great age that cannot deceive us, the most vivid and subtle discrimination of sense and the invention of images more powerful than sense.[116]

These descriptions capture perfectly the qualities of that other group of poet warriors who at that moment in Dublin were preparing to explode their art into the action of rebellion and to make out of their deaths an elaborate ritual. Pearse, MacDonagh, and Plunkett, in their lifelong pursuit of beauty certainly had more in common with Pater than with Achilles, and Yeats's description of the Japanese warriors holds true for Pearse and his comrades as well. MacDonagh, for example, was so taken with beauty that he wrote in a poem: "Fragment of a perfect plan / is the mortal life of man / Beauty alone can make it whole."[117] And Pearse was so obsessed with Cuchulain and the beauty he represented that he wrote articles and tracts under the pseudonym of Laegh Mac Riangabhra (Cuchulain's charioteer, who goaded him to greater bravery with taunts of cowardice).[118] Pearse finally gave up his profession as a barrister altogether to open a school (St. Endas) which would resemble the elite schools for young Celtic warriors described in the Irish sagas: "This man had kept a school / And rode our winged horse" ("Easter 1916," 24–25). The curriculum Pearse created was based on the aristocratic traditions of the boy corps at Eamhain Macha—the band of children of the famous, who, like Cuchulain, sat at the feet of the Druids and learned how to create exquisite poetry and to construct a beautiful and chivalrous society. The school's magazine, *An Macaomh*, was a perfect reflection of the school itself. Pearse wanted the magazine to be a rallying point for all those who would bring back again to Ireland "that Heroic Age which reserved the highest honour for the hero who had the most childlike heart, for the king who had the largest pity, and for the poet who visioned the truest image of beauty."[119]

Pearse's every movement was governed by the ideal of beauty he desired for Ireland. Ruth Dudley Edwards notes that Pearse was determined to give the students at St. Endas more than just a good education. He wanted to bring each soul amongst them to perfection, "because for every soul there is a perfection meant for it alone, and which it alone is capable of attaining."[120] In order to create an atmosphere conducive to the attainment of such perfection, Pearse made his school one of the most beautiful in Ireland. Stained glass windows were made especially for the school by Sara Purser. Jack Yeats and George Russell donated original paintings and Pearse's brother Willie created some interesting sculptures. The school—an old graceful manor house set amidst the green fields and rolling hills of County Dublin—was itself a symbol of beauty and refinement—the perfect sanctuary for the restoration of Gaelic culture. It was the ideal residence for Pearse, who, like Yeats, was one of "the last romantics" who "chose for theme / Traditional sanctity and loveliness" ("Coole Park and Ballylee, 1931," 41–42), and who, like Mishima and the Japanese warriors, wished to make out of his death the highest form of art.

Yeats was drawn to ancient Japanese culture and the Japanese Noh not merely because the expression of beauty he found there was subtle and refined, but because the Japanese, like the Irish, have a strange "poetry of death": "These Japanese poets, too, feel for tomb and wood the emotion, the sense of awe that our Gaelic-speaking country-people will sometimes show. . . ."[121] He adds that there is so much in the Noh plays that reminds him of Irish legends that he believes that Irish legends and beliefs at one time may have "differed little from those of the Shinto worshipper."[122] Yeats's references to Cuchulain's reincarnation in the General Post Office would certainly be in keeping with the Shintostic concept of post-mortal existence described by Saburo Sakai in *Samurai*. According to Sakai, the Samurai warrior who dies a heroic death will continue to exist in the spirit realm as a guardian warrior directing and guiding other noble warriors on earth. At the end of the *Tain*, just after Cuchulain has been buried, he begins his postmortal existence as a noble warrior like his Samurai counterpart: "The three times fifty queens that loved Cuchulain saw him appear in his Druid chariot, going through Emain Macha, and they could hear him singing the music of the Sidhe."[123]

Yeats's essay on the Noh plays and the aristocratic warrior class of Japan which produced them provides invaluable insight into his views on the beauty of heroic death, the connection between poetry and death, and the blending of art and action. And since all of these elements were present in the Easter Rising, the essay helps us to understand in a deeper way Yeats's perception of the Rising as a form of "terrible beauty" which reflected the stoic ideals of the warrior as well as the poetic ideals of the artist. Mishima, referring to the old Japanese ideal of a combination of letters and the martial arts, writes that action "perishes with the blossom" while "literature is an imperishable flower. And an imperishable flower, of course, is an artificial flower."[124] He concludes that to combine action and art is to combine the flower that wilts and the flower that lasts forever, to "blend within one individual the two most contradictory desires in humanity, and the respective dreams of those desires' realization."[125] The incongruous union of which Mishima speaks is dealt with in Yeats's description of Phase fifteen in *A Vision*. Yeats writes:

> Because the 15th Phase can never find direct human expression, being a supernatural incarnation, it impressed upon work and thought an element of strain and artifice, a desire to combine elements which may be incompatible, or which suggest by their combination something supernatural.[126]

Yeats writes that, during this phase, "intellect and emotion, primary curiosity and the antithetical dream, are for the moment one."[127] In 1916, "intellect and emotion, primary curiosity and the antithetical dream" were for the moment one. And in that moment "a terrible beauty" was born. The beauty is "terrible" because it has been achieved through the ultimate sacrifice—death.

Yeats stressed in the essay on the Noh that the ancient Japanese were more like the Irish than were the Greeks and Romans, "more like us even than Shakespeare and Corneille. Their emotion was self-conscious and reminiscent, always associating itself with pictures and poems."[128] These observations are significant with regard to the Easter Rebellion because both Yeats and the 1916 poets saw the Rising as the final piece in a mosaic whose rich design had been inspired by the images, pictures, and poems of Irish myth and legend. The landscape of Irish legend out of which the Mask of Cuchulain emerges, and the imaginative treatment of history found in Irish legend, form an artistic matrix which influenced the perception of the Rebellion by Yeats and the 1916 poets, for it was the legend of Irish history and not the fact of Irish history which Yeats and the 1916 poets found so irresistible, and which, in a sense, proved to be a catalyst to rebellion. Yeats had emphasized in *Autobiographies*, that you "cannot sum up a nation intellectually."[129] In Irish legend, Yeats found the perfect medium in which Ireland was summed up poetically and imagistically—a literary form or mask where "truth was embodied rather than actually known."[130]

Standish O'Grady, one of the great Irish Maskmakers, had approached Irish history in just this imaginative way in his *History of Ireland*. O'Grady so romantically illuminated that great "tapestry which hangs behind all of Irish history" that the story of Ireland becomes one great cosmic drama. His history begins "in the brooding anticipation of the silent instant before creation" on a landscape where "huge monsters, the as yet clumsy laboring of some inchoate passion yearning for expression, lumber across the stage of Pleistocene Ireland."[131] Across this frozen landscape pass an endless procession of "Gods, Fomorians, Firbolgs, and finally, the high Milesian race that is brought to consummate expression in its Hero, Cuchulain."[132]

O'Grady's imaginative approach to the Irish past proved irresistable to Yeats, since Yeats was not interested in a factual linear view of Irish history, but in an epiphanic one where the Image is predominant. Many of Yeats' poems and plays are, in a sense, an imaginative sequel to O'Grady's history, since they, like O'Grady's work, explore the legend of Irish history rather than the fact. According to Mary Helen Thuente, Yeats was drawn to Irish legend because of its disregard for strict historical accuracy and its symbolic depiction of reality.[133] Legend transcends history and time by depicting past events as simultaneous rather than successive. This was especially true of Irish oral tradition until the end of the nineteenth century, where there was not a strongly developed sense of the movement of time and the tendency was to compress the entire past into "one living yesterday."[134] As Thuente points out, Yeats's own work often represents a simultaneous rather than successive sense of time. This is particularly evident in his poem "The Black Tower", where he uses the present tense in the poem and thus narrates a "present medieval event."[135] Thuente notes that this tendency in Yeats can be traced to techniques he discovered in his early experience with Irish legends. In his Notes to "The Wanderings of Oisin," he describes this simultaneous sense of time:

The events it describes, like the events in most of the poems in this volume, are supposed to have taken place in the indefinite period, made up of many periods, described by the folk-tales, than in any particular century; it therefore, like the later Fenian stories themselves, mixes much that is medieval with much that is ancient.[136]

Similarly, he notes that in *The Countess Kathleen*, which he had based on a legend he had included in *Fairy and Folk Tales of the Irish Peasantry*, he "tried to suggest throughout the play that period, made out of many periods, in which the events of the folk-tales have happened."[137]

In legend, reality is transformed through the alchemy of the poetic imagination, and, just as alchemy distills the matter of the universe into its finest substance, legend presents men and women in their most passionate moments—their moments of greatest beauty. And in these moments, the greatest Masks are created. History thus becomes a series of illuminations of the human personality. When Yeats, in *A Vision*, identifies the definitive moments in history with the personalities of great men, he echoes the techniques of Irish legends. The beauty of Irish legend, "like all noble art," offers us "the mingling of contraries, the extremity of sorrow, the extremity of joy, perfection of personality, the perfection of surrender, overflowing turbulent energy, and marmorean stillness"[138]—all those contraries which find their ultimate expression in Cuchulain, precisely because he is the stuff of legend. Imagination has lifted Cuchulain out of history into the "timeless pattern" of legend and frozen his "turbulent energy" into the "marmorean stillness" of art. As an icon of "terrible beauty," he has become a symbol of all Irish warriors, all Irish poets, and all tragic lovers. He represents the tragic passion of Ireland itself, and as a national emblem in 1916 he proved irresistible.

Just as the scribe meticulously copied and embellished the ancient legends and the Irish bard carefully shaped the language of his poetry to reflect its content, so too Yeats in "Easter 1916" appears to be consciously shaping the rhythms of the poem to reflect its ancient heroism. Like the bards of ancient Ireland who recited in their verse the names of the heroic warriors killed in battle, Yeats "murmurs name upon name" (61) of the modern Irish warriors who died in 1916: "I write it out in a verse / MacDonagh and MacBride / And Connolly and Pearse" (34–36). Moreover, Robert O'Driscoll, in *An Ascendancy of the Heart*, points out that to conclude a line of verse with three monosyllabic feet was a distinctive feature of Gaelic bardic verse.[139] Many of the lines in "Easter 1916" end with three monosyllabic feet: "I have met them at close of day," "And thought before I had done," "Around the fire at the club"—these are just a few examples of this pattern but there are many more. Since Yeats was in the habit of choosing the rhythms of his language to suit his subject and based a great deal of his verse on the traditional meters of the old bardic schools and the rhythms of Gaelic folksongs, it is highly likely that he consciously shaped the language of the poem to reflect its heroic subject. Michael Yeats, in "W. B. Yeats and Irish

Folksong," discusses the influence of Gaelic folksongs on his father's work,[140] and Sean Lucy has demonstrated how Yeats in "The Cold Heaven" achieved a perfect counterpoint of rhythms by mounting the stress lines of the Gaelic *amhran* or "song poetry" on a regular iambic line.[141] Yeats himself, in "A General Introduction for my Work," tells us that he was especially concerned with choosing the appropriate meter to reflect the Irish Heroic Age: "Our Heroic Age went better, or so I fancied, in the ballad metre of *The Green Helmet*. There was something in what I felt about Deirdre, about Cuchulain that rejected the Renaissance and its characteristic metres."[142] It seems highly likely, therefore, that in "Easter 1916" Yeats consciously uses the old Bardic meter to perpetuate the "legend" of the Rising and to celebrate in "ancient" rhythms the greatness of modern warriors reliving an ancient myth. Yeats makes it clear that it is the "legend" of the Rising and its connection with other legends that fascinates him, and not the historical "fact":

> I was in Dublin a little later and I found everyone talking of the last moments of the executed men. Some of the fine things had been said and done but many were legends. Dublin cynicism had passed away and was inventing beautiful, instead of derisive, fables. They told me Madame Markiewicz had kissed her revolver when she surrendered, that the officer who witnessed Pearse's execution said that he died like a prince. . . .[143]

ii

To begin to understand the Rising, then, and Yeats's perception of it as part of an ongoing legend of terrible beauty, one must examine not only the symbols and images which form the dramatic backdrop of the Rising (as Thompson does) but the complex imaginative processes which gave birth to those symbols, and the search for beauty and self-sacrifice which was the driving power behind the creation of such images. One must get back to what Yeats describes as "the aboriginal ice"[144] behind Irish legend. Charles Donahue, referring to the imagistic world of Celtic Christianity, writes:

> The world of early Irish Christianity cannot be understood . . . in terms of 'ideas' or the history of ideas. It is a world of symbolic theology where the investigator who would understand must work with images rather than abstract concepts.[145]

Just as the world of Irish Insular Christianity cannot be understood in terms of ideas or the history of ideas, so too the Irish "insular" world of the Easter Rebellion cannot be understood in the terms of abstract political ideology or in the terms of Freudian psychology, with which Thompson identifies it. The world of Irish politics in 1916 was, like the early Celtic Church, steeped in "symbolic theology," and the Masks which accompanied that theology owed their lineaments not to Freud and modern psychology but to the archetypal images and poetic traditions of the Gaelic past. Mask and Image played such a critical part in the liturgy of the Rising that Father F. X. Martin, in "Myth, Fact, and Mystery," writes that the Rebellion was "staged consciously as a drama by its principal actors,"[146] and Yeats refers to its participants as dramatic players:

> Who was the first man shot that day?
> the player Connolly
> Close to the City Hall he died;
> Carriage and voice had he;
> He lacked those years that go with skill
> But later might have been
> a famous, a brilliant figure
> Before that painted scene.
>
> ("Three Songs to the One Burden," 64–71)

Yeats's use of the phrase "painted scene" suggests not only Connolly's aborted theatrical career on the stage, but his aborted career in the "dramatic" arena of Irish politics—an arena filled from time immemorial with richly painted scenes. He uses the same phrase to describe the flamboyant lifestyle of Oscar Wilde. Wilde, Yeats writes, turned the "easel-painting" of his masters into the "painted scenes" of his own life, and the quality of Wilde's "aesthetically" arranged life suggested to Yeats some "deliberate artistic composition."[147] In Pearse and the other executed poets, Yeats obviously saw the same tendency to pose or wear a Mask that he saw in Wilde. It is interesting that the only other time Yeats uses the phrase "terrible beauty" outside of "Easter 1916" is to describe a short story Wilde had written about outcasts who are doomed despite the fact that Christ has raised them up. Yeats felt the story reflected the tragic quality of Wilde's own life and death:

> Wilde published that story a little later, but spoiled it with the verbal decoration of his epoch, and I have to repeat it to myself as I first heard it, before I can see its terrible beauty. I no more doubt its sincerity than I doubt that his parade of gloom, all that late rising and sleeping away his life, that elaborate playing with tragedy, was an attempt to escape from an emotion by its exaggeration.[148]

Yeats saw Wilde's aesthetic Mask as an attempt to create in art all he had missed in life. He felt that Wilde "lived with no self-mockery at all, an imaginary life, perpetually performed a play which was in all things the opposite of all that he had known in childhood and early youth,"[149] and thus was that life's antithesis.

When one considers the terms of artifice which Yeats uses to describe the Rebellion and its participants, it becomes obvious that his doctrine of the Mask plays a central role in his perception of the Rebellion as theater and its participants as players. His references to the Rebellion suggest that he sees the rebels as artists who created out of the Rising "a deliberate artistic composition." Describing some of the characteristics of the ritual theater of Masks he wished to establish, Yeats once wrote: ". . . the actors must move, for the most part slowly and quietly, and there should be something in their movements decorative and rhythmical, as if they were paintings on a frieze."[150] In "Easter 1916" Yeats seems to be trying to achieve this effect in verse. By his emphatic use of the demonstrative adjective to point out to the reader, one by one, the individual patriots in the drama, one gets the feeling that the narrator of the poem is pointing to figures which are like "paintings in a frieze"—figures which have already been changed "changed utterly" by the Mask of Art:

> That woman's days were spent
> In ignorant good-will. . . .
> This man had kept a school
> And rode our winged horse;
> This other his helper and friend
> Was coming into his force. . . .
> This other man I had dreamed
> A drunken, vainglorious lout.
> ("Easter 1916," 17–18, 24–27, 31–32)

The rebels consciously create their own icon by embracing the Mask of Cuchulain and willing their own deaths. In "Per Amica Silentia Lunae" Yeats wrote: ". . . active virtue as distinguished from the passive acceptance of a code, is . . . theatrical, consciously dramatic, the wearing of a Mask."[151] By consciously choosing a heroic death, the rebels have entered Phase fifteen of Yeats's lunar cycle. Yeats describes this phase as one of "Complete Beauty" where the Body of Fate is dissolved in the Mask and the soul has died "into the labryinth of itself" (p. 164). In *A Vision*, Yeats described the Mask as the "antiself or opposite of the Will. It is the image of what we wish to become, or of that to which we give our reverence."[152] In death, the rebels have become one with the image of Cuchulain they revered and have finally achieved the elusive beauty they sought. Michael Robartes, in "The Phases of the Moon," describes this type of experience:

> All thought becomes an image and the soul
> Becomes a body: that body and that soul
> Too perfect at the full to lie in a cradle,
> Too lonely for the traffic of the world:

Body and soul cast out and cast away
Beyond the visible world.

(58–63)

The three poems "Easter 1916," "Sixteen Dead Men," and "The Rose
Tree" appear to be structured around this experience. In the poems "all
thought becomes an image" as the poet moves from the primary world of flux
which we encounter at the beginning of each poem to the completely
antithetical world of art and death that we encounter at the end. All three
poems begin with the chaos of words and end in the silent stasis of image. In
"Easter 1916," for example, Yeats tells us at the beginning of the poem, that
in the past when he met the rebels he uttered "polite meaningless words"
(6). By the third stanza of the poem, however, all words and movements have
been replaced by the hard cold image of the stone—"The stone's in the midst
of all"—which dominates the poem from that point on. Yeats mentions the
stone three times in the last two stanzas and then immediately recites the
names of the executed rebels who, through the Mask of death, have moved
"beyond the visible world" and assumed the cold final beauty of stone
themselves.

The stone which is the central metaphor of the poem is one of Yeats's
"masterful images" and has mythological and nationalistic associations that
can be traced back to the dawn of Irish history. These associations give it a
depth and resonance far beyond its immediate metaphorical implications.
Yeats scholars see the stone as a symbol of rigidity and death[153]—a reflection
of the fanatic dedication of the rebels to their political ideals. And although
the stone symbol does, indeed, effectively suggest the hypnotic devotion of
the rebels to the Irish Cause—"Too long a sacrifice / Can make a stone of the
heart," it also suggests much more. The stone appears to represent Ireland
herself, for one of the well-known names of Ireland, Inisfail ("Island of the
Stone of Destiny"), was, as Geoffrey Keating tells us, derived from the name
Lia Fail ("the Stone of Destiny").[154] The Stone of Destiny was one of the four
sacred talismans of the Tuatha De Danaan ("people of the Goddess Dana"),
who came to Ireland before the dawn of Irish history. All the kings of Ireland,
both pagan and Christian, were crowned upon this stone, and their destiny
was tied in with its magical powers. Keating notes that, besides being
"enchanted," the stone also had "fatal" qualities and was described by
Hector Boethius as "saxum fatale."[155] In other words, the stone possessed
the "terrible beauty" of Ireland herself. As mentioned earlier, the first elegy
written in Ireland refers to a beautiful but "fatal" Milesian goddess named
"Fail." Thus, from its earliest origins, Ireland has been linked with both a
"fatal" stone and a "fatal" woman whose name is intimately linked with that
stone. Significantly, six years before the Easter Rising, Yeats, as if recalling
the "fatal" qualities of the Lia Fail, turns to the image of the stone to reflect
the Mask of implacable rigidity that Ireland sometimes wore: "The Soul of

Ireland is a vapour and her body a stone."[156] And in "Poetry and Tradition," Yeats refers to Inisfail and the fatal destiny of those who try to free her:

> A dream! a dream! an ancient dream!
> Yet, ere peace come to Inisfail,
> Some weapons on some field must gleam,
> Some burning glory fire the Gael.[157]

Yeats, of course, was fully aware of the origins of the name, *Inisfail* and was thoroughly familiar with the history of the Stone of Destiny. In the extensive "Notes" to his poem "Baile and Aillinn," for example, Yeats discusses the origins of the Lia Fail and its connection with Falias, the mysterious city from which the Lia Fail derived its name and from which in turn the name of Ireland (Inisfail) evolved:

> And Findrias and Falias and Gorias and Murias were the four mysterious cities whence the Tuatha De Danaan, the divine race, came to Ireland, cities of learning out of sight of the world, there they found their four talismans, the Spear, the Stone, the Cauldron, and the Sword.[158]

Yeats's short stories, furthermore, are filled with references to the Lia Fail. The stories "Red Hanrahan," "The Death of Hanrahan," and "Rosa Alchemica" revolve around the Stone of Destiny and the three other Irish talismans, and in the first two stories Yeats explores both the "enchanted" and the "fatal" qualities of the Stone mentioned by Keating. In "Red Hanrahan," the poet Hanrahan is hypnotized by the fatal beauty of Echtge—a woman of the Sidhe who lures him away from his human sweetheart to ecstasy and doom. Echtge clearly represents Ireland herself, for she is connected in the story with the Stone of Destiny, and, like Ireland under British rule, she has lain for a long time asleep awaiting a virile poet to awaken her.[159] In "The Death of Hanrahan," Hanrahan, immediately following the ecstatic consummation of his marriage to a woman who is possessed by the Sidhe, cries out the names of the four talismans just before he dies: ". . . and he said very loud and clear, 'The Cauldron, the Stone, the Sword, the Spear. What are they? Who do they belong to?' . . . And then he fell back again, weak, and the breath going from him."[160]

Yeats's fascination with the Stone of Destiny filled both his writings and his personal life. Accompanied by Maud Gonne, Yeats visited the actual site of the Stone of Destiny at Tara and for years was obsessed with the idea of creating an Irish Mystical Order using a replica of the Stone as one of its central talismans. He insisted that the cult should meet in a castle built of Irish stone with the replica of the Lia Fail serving as the Altar.[161]

As a national, mythological, and personal symbol, then, the Stone of Destiny has been woven into the fabric of Yeats's life and work. That such an ancient image would prove to be such a hypnotic and enduring symbol for

Yeats is not surprising, for Yeats revered ancient symbols and wrote of their evocative power in "Symbolism in Poetry":

> If I look at the moon herself and remember any of her ancient names and meanings, I move among divine people, and things that have shaken off our mortality, the tower of ivory, the Queen of waters, the shining stag among enchanted woods. . . .[162]

Yeats also wrote: "A great work of Art . . . is as rooted in the early ages as the Mass which goes back to savage folk-lore. . . ."[163] The Stone of Destiny, "rooted" in the very landscape of Ireland with its prehistoric burial chambers, cairn-crowned hills, and druidic ruins, is an inextricable part of that tapestry of "ancient names" Yeats mentions. Given Yeats's interest in the Stone of Destiny and its national implications, it is highly likely that in "Easter 1916," Yeats intended the stone symbol to suggest that more "ancient" stone at Tara, and, by extension, the fatal beauty of Ireland, herself: "Hearts with one purpose alone / Through summer and winter seem / Enchanted to a stone." Ireland is the "enchanted" but "fatal" stone that's "in the midst of all":

> We know their dream; enough
> To know they dreamed and are dead;
> And what if excess of love
> Bewildered them till they died?
> I write it out in a verse—
> MacDonagh and MacBride
> And Connolly and Pearse
> Now and in time to be,
> Wherever green is worn,
> Are changed, changed utterly:
> A terrible beauty is born.
>
> (70–80)

The movement from words to Image that we see in "Easter 1916" is repeated in "Sixteen Dead Men," where Yeats tells us in the first two lines of the poem: "O but we talked at large before / the sixteen men were shot" (1–2), then dramatically shows us the impotence of words when confronted with the powerful images of the dead: "And is their logic to outweigh / MacDonagh's bony thumb?" (11–12). The poem ends in the antithetical world of Phase fifteen where the rebels converse, not in the futile words of the "primary" world, but "bone to bone" (18). Yeats may have taken this phrase from Pearse's poem "The Rebel," written shortly before his death. In the poem, Pearse, referring to the Irish people, declares, "I am bone of their bone."[164]

 "The Rose Tree" follows the same pattern of movement as the other two poems. The first stanza of the poem emphasizes the futility of words:

"O words are lightly spoken,"
Said Pearse to Connolly,
"Maybe a breath of politic words
Has withered our Rose Tree;
Or maybe but a wind that blows
Across the bitter sea."

(1–6)

And by the last stanza, the rebels have moved away from the chaos of the primary world, away from the "wind that blows / Across the bitter sea," and from the confusion of "politic words" into the awful serenity of death. The poem ends with the transcendent Image of the antithetical world—the Image of the Rose. In *A Vision*, the symbol which Yeats assigns to Phase fifteen, the phase of perfect beauty, is the "Rose of Beatitude,"[165] and, in "The Rose Tree," this symbol represents Ireland beatified by the sacrificial blood of the rebels.

Morton Seiden, in *The Poet as a Mythmaker*, writes that in "Easter 1916," "Sixteen Dead Men," and "The Rose Tree" Yeats transforms the entire drama of the Easter Rising into an archaic ritual of sacrifice which is a blend of Gaelic heliolatry and Orphic rite.[166] In Gaelic heliolatry the reborn earth god is associated with the revolving year and the dying and reborn day, and in Gaelic and Orphic nature myth there is a ritual murder of a god whose annual death and rebirth symbolize the changing seasons. As Seiden points out, in "Easter 1916," the death of the rebels was the result of "too long a sacrifice," yet a sacrifice out of which "a terrible beauty is born," just as the year itself is now being reborn at Eastertide 1916.[167] In "Sixteen Dead Men" the rebels are alive again in Anima Mundi where they "converse bone to bone." Finally, in "The Rose Tree," the sacrificial blood of the men brings new life to the parched land, makes "the green come out again" and creates "a right Rose Tree." The Christian overtones of Christ's passion, death, and resurrection at Easter are also obvious in the three poems, and the pagan-Christian synthesis is exactly what Yeats would have intended, for he wished to create for Ireland a Mask which would blend Druid and Christian mysteries: "I did not think . . . this would be altogether pagan, for it was plain that its symbols must be selected from all those things that have moved men most during many, mainly Christian centuries."[168]

Yeats had marveled at this pagan-Christian synthesis in his discussion of the great Irish tapestry in "A General Introduction for my Work," and he had seen how the poet rebels, in their adoption of the Cuchulain Mask, had added a few traces of Christian color to its pagan lineaments. Furthermore, as a member of the Golden Dawn, Yeats had witnessed this fascinating synthesis first hand. The exotic ceremonies of the Hermetic Students of the Golden Dawn were based on the symbols and rituals of many different religions, both pagan and Christian. The most important ritual of the Order was the Rebirth Ritual. The adept symbolically died or killed himself and was reborn as Dionysus, Christ, Orpheus, or a fourteenth century adept by the name of Father Christian Rosenkrantz; his rebirth symbolized the alchemist's transmutation of matter into its divine counterpart, as well as his own ascent of the Sephirotic Tree of Life to God.[169] The Order delighted in ceremony, ritual, and symbol, and one of their most important symbols, which frequently appears in Yeats's early works, was a red rose superimposed on a cross. This cross signified time and eternity, love and sacrifice, and the resolved antinomies[170]—all those things which intersected at the sacrifice of Easter 1916.

In the rituals of the Golden Dawn, Yeats discovered analogues to what he had discovered in Celtic and Greek myth. As Israel Regardie points out, the Hermetic Students saw the rebirth ritual as an archetypal symbol of all circles and all antinomies. This ritual was based on the three essential themes of Celtic and Greek myth: the ritual murder, the death and resurrection of nature deities, the revolving seasons and the waxing and waning day. In the nineties when Yeats was contemplating the creation of an Irish Mystical Order, he planned to incorporate into its doctrines much that he had learned in the Golden Dawn. The rituals were to be based on Celtic heliolatry, but Celtic heliolatry colored by the Orphic Mysteries, the philosophy of Shelley and Blake, and of the Theosophists and the Hermetic Students. The purpose of the Order was to bring together Gaelic and Greek myth, national politics, and various other exotic religions in an effort to effect a spiritual regeneration of the modern Celt.[171]

Although the Irish Mystical Order never materialized, the "terrible beauty" of the Easter Rebellion did bring about, at least momentarily, the spiritual regeneration of the modern Celt. Yeats's exposure to Celtic Ritual as a member of the Golden Dawn, furthermore, provided him with the images and themes of ritual sacrifice which he uses in "Easter 1916," "Sixteen Dead Men," and "The Rose Tree" to connect the modern "sacrifice" of Easter 1916 with the ancient sacrifices of pagan Ireland.

As a member of the Golden Dawn, Yeats was exposed not only to the rich language of the symbolic sacrificial rituals, but to the Masking ceremonies which formed an important part of those rituals. And in addition to the influence of Wilde, Blake, Madame Blavatsky, Dowden[172] and others upon Yeats's ever expanding doctrine of the Mask, these ceremonies must have played an important part in the development of his complex theory. The members of the Golden Dawn saw the Mask as an image of the idealized selfhood to which the adept aspired. And, significantly, the adept wore an actual Mask during the initiation ceremony. This Mask served as a symbol of the Higher Self or God the adept might eventually become.[173] This concept of Sacrificial Mask is central to the role played by Mask in the Easter Rising, both in Yeats's perception of the Cuchulain Mask embraced by the rebels and the perception of the rebels themselves regarding their own Masks. Although one cannot say for certain that Yeats's doctrine of the Mask directly influenced Pearse and his fellow poets regarding their own concept of Mask, the uncanny similarities between their ideas about the Mask and Yeats's theories suggest that it did. The 1916 poets acknowledge Yeats's literary influence on them in many areas—Thomas MacDonagh dedicated a book of his poetry to Yeats and sought Yeats's advice on poetry generally. Johann Norstedt points out that Yeats's influence is easily discernible in Mac-Donagh's poems and plays.[174] And Pearse acknowledged his debt to Yeats on many occasions. Furthermore, since Pearse and his fellow poets frequently came into contact with Yeats in connection with the Irish Dramatic Movement, it is almost impossible to imagine that they would not have been familiar with his views on Mask and theater.

The theme of sacrifice pervades the poetry, plays, and prose of the 1916 poets, as does a fascination with Mask and Image. MacDonagh, in his poem "Of the Man of my First Play," for example, asks if the contemplative poet can fill the heroic "Mask" of the revolutionary:

> How may I show him? How his story plan
> Who was prefigured to the dreaming eye
> In term of other being? May he fill
> This Mask of life? Or will my creature cry
> Shame that I dwarf the sequel and the man
> To house him thus within a fragment still.[175]

MacDonagh is referring here to Turlough the poet patriot of his play *When the Dawn is Come,* which was accepted by Yeats and Synge for a performance at the Abbey Theatre in October 1908. The play centers on the psychological dualism inherent in the role of poet patriot and the courage required by the poet who wished to don the heroic Mask. The play ends with the tragic death of the young poet. And, as Johan Norstedt points out in his biography of MacDonagh, the play echoes the note of tragedy in MacDonagh's poems, which celebrate the deaths of young poets for a patriotic cause.[176] The play also reflects MacDonagh's own personal struggle between his role as poet on the one hand and revolutionary on the other. MacDonagh's son Donagh claims that his father foretold his own fate in this play.[177] Both poem and play reflect Yeats's doctrine of the Antithetical Mask, as described by him in "Per Amica Silentia Lunae":

Daimon comes not as like to like but seeking its own opposite, for man and Daimon feed the hunger in one another's hearts. Because the ghost is simple, the man heterogeneous and confused, they are but knit together when the man has found a mask whose lineaments permit the expression of all the man most lacks, and it may be dreads, and of that only.[178]

In the heroic Mask of "that violent man Cuchulain," MacDonagh found the Mask whose "lineaments" permitted the expression of all he most lacked and dreaded, just as Turlough the poet finds in the lineaments of the revolutionary Mask his own opposite. In daily life, MacDonagh was not a dashing man of action but a poet and academic, and he had once studied to be a priest. He was Assistant Professor of English at University College, Dublin, and, although he led the Second Battalion of the Irish Volunteers into Jacob's biscuit factory on Easter Monday, he was more at home amid the intricacies of language than fighting in a rebellion. This was the man of whom Yeats had written in "Easter 1916": "So sensitive his nature seemed, / So daring and sweet his thought" (29–30). His very love of the Irish language, however, is what led him to assume the heroic Mask in 1916, and his road to the firing squad lay in the Irish language revival movement. He once write that "the Gaelic revival has given to some of us a new arrogance" and added: " 'Gaedheal me agus ni heol dom gur nair dom e'—I am a Gael and I know no cause but of pride in that."[179]

MacDonagh's determination to embrace his Antithetical Mask—to unite blood with vision, and to live the heroic myths he had read and written about—is revealed in the climactic speech of Fitzmaurice in MacDonagh's play *Pagans*, where he refers to the poet as being "double-lived":

> My writings have been only the prelude to my other work. . . . I have long regretted that I have not in my time had an opportunity of doing something worthwhile, and now it is here. . . . I am going to live the things that I have before imagined. It is well for a poet that he is double-lived. He has two stores of power. You will not know yourself in the Ireland that we shall make here. . . .[180]

When Fitzmaurice asserts that he and his comrades will "make" Ireland, he is expressing the ideas of MacDonagh, the "conscious" craftsman who sees himself as a creator of beauty. Like Plato's skillful carpenter in Book 10 of *The Republic*[181] who makes a bed based on his idea of what the perfect bed should be, MacDonagh and his fellow poets set out to carve a Mask for Ireland based on the perfect images of Ireland they had seen in Irish literature. Like Yeats, who tells us that, when he remakes a poem, "it is myself I remake,"[182] MacDonagh and his fellow poets will attempt to remake both themselves and Ireland through their poetry and their deaths.

Regarding his own individual Mask, MacDonagh was not exaggerating when he said that "I am going to live the things that I have before imagined," for MacDonagh, like Oscar Wilde, became so enamored of his chosen Mask that he began to dress the part the Mask dictated. In the years preceding the Rebellion he became well known for his dramatic posturing in the green uniform of the Irish Volunteers at recruiting drives and training sessions. In 1916, the drama grew more intense. During one of his lectures at University College, he exhibited a revolver and at a sidewalk rally he dramatically drew a sword.[183]

The sword, like the Stone of Destiny, is one of the major symbols in the

Irish tapestry. The Tuatha de Danaan brought with them to Ireland, along with the Stone of Destiny, three other talismans, among them the Sword of Light (An Claideamh Soluis).[184] The sword later became the symbol of the warrior Cuchulain, and, in the fresco which stood over the entrance to St. Endas where MacDonagh taught for a while, the boy hero Cuchulain is depicted with sword drawn, ready to take arms for the first time. In 1907, Yeats, using the traditional symbol of the sword, had said of the Irish Literary Movement: "We were to forge in Ireland a new sword on our old traditional anvil for that great battle that must in the end re-establish the old, confident, joyous world."[185] And in "Estrangement," he defined supreme art as a "traditional statement of certain heroic and religious truths, passed on from age to age, modified by individual genius, but never abandoned."[186]

MacDonagh's fascination with the symbols and emblems of ancient Ireland which signified those "traditional . . . heroic and religious truths" Yeats speaks of was total. Once, after a performance of Pearse's Cuchulain pageant by his St. Endas pupils, MacDonagh marched with the student actors through the streets of Dublin holding the school banner adorned with the gold sun disc of the Fianna. Many of the students held ancient battleaxes borrowed from the school museum, while others held tall gilded spears which shone in the lamp-lit streets. The effect was startling and a crowd began to follow them singing a popular ballad about the rebellion of 1798. MacDonagh was so excited as the crowd swelled to the dimensions of a riot that he declared, "Egad! they expect us to lead them against the Castle."[187]

Needless to say, MacDonagh's sense of Mask and Image was heightened by dramatic processions such as this, and also by his appearance as an actor in Pearse's heroic dramas. MacDonagh's desire to turn all to Mask and Image is evident in the following stanza from his poem "Wishes for My Son," where the frenzy of battle has been transformed into the stylized Image of the dance:

> Wild and perilous holy things
> Flaming with the martyr's blood
> And the joy that laughs and sings
> Where a foe must be withstood
> Joy of headlong happy chance
> Leading on the battle dance.[188]

In April 1916, while MacDonagh and his fellow poets were preparing to don the heroic Masks for the "battle dance" of the Easter Rising, Yeats was discussing in his essay on Japanese drama the stylized movements of the Noh Play, the Japanese drama of Masks. In the essay, Yeats discusses the Japanese technique of portraying the battle as a dance:

At the climax, instead of the disordered passion of nature, there is a dance, a series of positions and movements which may represent a battle. . . .

The interest is not in the human form but in the rhythm to which it moves, and the triumph of their art is to express the rhythm in its intensity.[189]

Before 1916, MacDonagh knew as little as Yeats about the "disordered passion" of real battles and, like Yeats, was more drawn to the "stylized" battles of art than the real battles of blood and terror. Many of the poems, therefore, in which he celebrates battle like a seasoned warrior are but Masks which represent in aesthetic form an Image of all that he lacks and fears most. His poems are a perfect reflection of Yeats's theory that an artist's creations are often reflections of his Antithetical Mask. Yeats expresses his poetic theory about the relationship between the antithetical Mask and creative art in "Ego Dominus Tuus," where Ille tells us that Dante "set his chisel to the hardest stone" by fashioning "from his opposite / An image" of art. Dante, who according to Yeats, led a lecherous life, created in his art, an Image or Mask of perfect purity—"the most exalted lady loved by a man":

> Being mocked by Guido for his lecherous life,
> Derided and deriding, driven out
> To climb that stair and eat that bitter bread,
> He found the unpersuadable justice, he found
> The most exalted lady loved by a man.
>
> (32–36)

And Keats, who was poor and in ill health, created opulent images and joyful song:

> His art is happy, but who knows his mind?
> I see a schoolboy when I think of him,
> With face and nose pressed to a sweet-shop window
> For certainly he sank into the grave
> His senses and his heart unsatisfied,
> And made—being poor, ailing and ignorant
> Shut out from all the luxury of the world,
> The coarse-bred son of a livery-stable keeper—
> Luxuriant song.
>
> (54–62)

The "Luxuriant Song" of MacDonagh, which celebrates the great battles of Ireland's epic heroes in "tapestries of gold"[190] and other opulent images, is an attempt to transform the "blood and mire of human veins" into the stasis of art—to diminish the horror of death by enfolding it within the beauty of art and to prepare himself for 1916 and the Antithetical Mask which was his opposite.

Plunkett, too, in his poetry, transforms the blood of battle into the exquisite image of the tapestry: "Far have you flown and blows of battle cease / To drape the skies in tapestries of blood."[191] Plunkett's lush poetry masks his delicate health. Like Keats, he was suffering from consumption, and, like Keats, he celebrates life in the most luxuriant of images:

> Crowns and imperial purple, thrones of gold,
> Onyx and sard and blazing diadems,
> Lazuli and hyacinth and powerful gems
> Undreamt of even in Babylon of old
> May for a price be given, bought and sold,
> Bartered for silver as was Bethlehehm's
> And yet a Splendour lives that price contemns
> Since Five loud Tongues a deeper worth have told.[192]

It is ironic that a poem ablaze with such exotic color was written by a man with failing health and very weak eyesight. Like Dante, Plunkett "set his chisel to the hardest stone." Much harder than the creation of one's Antithetical Mask in art, however, is the adoption of one's Antithetical Mask in life, and Plunkett achieved this through his adoption of the Cuchulain Mask in the Easter Rebellion. Plunkett, like MacDonagh, was not exactly the modern counterpart of the strong virile warrior. Pale and delicate, Plunkett was a mystic and a great lover of poetry. He was the son of a papel count, and Goddard Lieberson describes him as being a gentle, sensitive young man, whose ill health forced him to travel abroad to Sicily, Malta, and Algeria in the hope of finding a cure.[193] He was quite ill when he fought in the Easter Rebellion. Peter McBrien writes that, in order to take part in the Rising, Plunkett actually got up from his bed in a hospital where he had just undergone an operation.[194] In spite of this, however, Plunkett embraced his heroic Mask was a passion equal to that of Cuchulain, ending his short life in a blaze of glory. Pale and emaciated, his throat covered in bandages from his recent operation and his hands glittering with rings,[195] he strode into the Post Office with sword in hand, looking very much like a hero from some ancient saga.

Plunkett, who had a flair for the theatrical and had directed many of Pearse's heroic dramas, was obviously drawn to the idea of the Mask. He even wrote a poem called "The Mask," which may have been influenced by Yeats's poem of the same name. In the poem, he speaks of a woman "wearing a dreadful mask", behind which her eyes are "as still as death and cold."[196] His own death Mask, by contrast, was a flame of burning passion and his own life the perfect embodiment of Yeats's doctrine of the Mask in that he was "consciously dramatic." Instead of passively accepting his illness and living the life of an invalid, he deliberately chose a Mask whose Dionysian energy provided a dramatic contrast to his own frailty. In *A Vision*, Yeats describes the Antithetical Mask as a "form created by passion to unite us to ourselves."[197] This was certainly true of Plunkett's Mask, for his extravagant passions transcended the limitations of his illness and allowed him to achieve Unity of Being through his Antithetical Mask.

Padraic Pearse, like his fellow poets, embraced his Antithetical Mask during the Easter Rebellion. Pearse, who was proclaimed President of the Provisional Government and Commander-in-Chief of the Army of the Republic, was not an experienced military leader like Major MacBride, but a poet and teacher. It was "the fascination of what's difficult" that led Pearse to choose a Mask that was his antithesis. The following words spoken by Ille in "Ego Dominus Tuus," could easily have been spoken by Pearse in the Post Office: "By the help of an image / I call to my own opposite, summon all / That I have handled least, least looked upon" (7–9). These lines answer Yeats's question in his poem "The Statues," "When Pearse summoned Cuchulain to his side / What stalked through the Post Office?" The spirit of Cuchulain that Pearse summoned to his side, was Pearse's own anti-self, his Antithetical Mask, for Mary Colum has described Pearse's daily self as being the opposite of the stoic warrior. Pearse, Colum observes, was "gentle and shy in conversation."[198] When in the presence of large masses of people, however, he became imperious and masterful, she adds, and his strength and passion were sometimes overwhelming.[199] In *An Barr Buadh*, Pearse once wrote to himself, "I suppose there are two Pearses, the sombre and taciturn Pearse and the gay and sunny Pearse."[200] And the Abbey actress Marie ni Shiubhlaigh, describing the duality of Pearse's personality remarked: "Inside St. Endas he was a quiet young man, full of nothing but the business of the school. But outside, some might have said Pearse was vain—a bit of a 'poseur.'"[201]

In an autobiographical fragment, Pearse once wrote that he was driven by two disparate purposes: "a deep homing instinct" and an "impulse to seek hard things to do, to go on far quests and fight for lost causes."[202] But, as Raymond Porter points out, these forces were not so cross-purposed as Pearse thought, for the Gaelic League, the Irish Volunteers, educational reform, the Easter Rising of 1916—all were "hard things to do," "far quests," and "lost causes." But they were also reflections of a nation's desire and need for roots, a nation's "homing instinct."[203] The two impulses that Pearse recognized in his nature, working in "fruitful" opposition to each other, created a dynamic synthesis which accounts for the life he led and the death he died in front of a British firing squad on 3 May 1916.[204] Pearse's heroic Antithetical Mask, which was reflected in his desire "to go on far quests and fight for lost causes," was blended with the daily self which can be seen in his "deep homing instinct."

Pearse, like Yeats, had a theory about the human personality and the call to heroic action, and he identified with those for whom heroic action was not easy or natural, but, as Yeats writes in his descriptions of the Antithetical Mask, "the greatest obstacle they must confront without despair."[205] The following excerpt from a speech given by Pearse contains ideas which are remarkably similar to ideas expressed in Yeats's Doctrine of the Mask:

It is easy to imagine how the spirit of Irish patriotism called to the gallant and adventurous spirit of Tone or moved the wrathful spirit of Mitchel. In them deep called unto deep; heroic effort claimed the heroic man. But consider how the call was made to a spirit of different, yet not less noble mould; and how it was answered. In Emmet it called to a dreamer and he awoke a man of action; it called to a student and a recluse, and he awoke a man of action; it called to one who loved the ways of peace and he became a revolutionary. . . .[206]

When Pearse writes that Emmet, who was a dreamer, "awoke a man of action" and that he "who loved the ways of peace" awoke a revolutionary, he is referring to an individual who, according to Yeats's theory, has chosen his Antithetical Mask. Pearse's description of Emmet as a "dreamer" who "awoke a man of action," holds true for Pearse as well. And Pearse's poem "Renunciation" reflects the difficulty experienced by the dreamer who must reject the seductive beauty of the world of which he is so enamored in order to embrace the more terrible, transfiguring beauty of death. Written in 1915, the poem anticipates Pearse's death:

> Naked I saw thee,
> O beauty of beauty,
> And I blinded my eyes
> For fear I should fail.
>
> I heard thy music,
> O melody of melody,
> And I closed my ears
> For fear I should falter.
>
> . . . .
>
> I turned my back
> On the vision I had shaped
> And to this road before me
> I turned my face.
>
> I have turned my face
> To this road before me
> To the deed that I see
> And the death I shall die.[207]

iii

The poets of 1916, then, reflected in a remarkable way Yeats's doctrine of the Mask. In his letter to Ethel Mannin which was discussed in Chapter 1, Yeats had written that, if a man's life is successful and he escapes "mere mass death," he can achieve Unity of Being through his death and that all men with "subjective" natures "move toward a possible ecstasy." In *Autobiographies*, he defines "subjective" men as all those who must "spin a web out of their own bowels,"[208] and he writes that their "victory is an intellectual daily re-creation of all that exterior fate snatches away, and so that fate's antithesis."[209] He adds that "what I have called 'The Mask' is an emotional antithesis to all that comes out of their internal nature."[210] Pearse and his fellow poets were "subjective" and triumphant because, although "exterior fate" snatched away their lives, they made poetry out of their deaths. They escaped "mere mass death" not only by dedicating their lives to a noble ideal, but by assuming the heroic Mask at the moment of death. Of such individuals and their art, Yeats writes in "Hodos Chameliontos":

> We gaze at such men in awe, because we gaze not at a work of art, but at the re-creation of the man through the art, the birth of a new species of man, and, it may even seem that the hairs of our heads stand up, because that birth, that re-creation, is from terror. Had not Dante and Villon understood that their fate wrecked what life could not rebuild, they could but have found a false beauty . . . and suffered no change at all.[211]

The 1916 poets "re-created" themselves and Ireland not only through the Mask of Art, but also through the Mask of Death. Like Dante and Villon, they understood perfectly that "their fate wrecked what life could not rebuild." And they knew that, before they could pass forever into the sphere of art, they must face the real "terror" of the firing squads. They knew that, when the curtain of Rebellion was brought down, that "terror" would come quickly enough. They were right—the British showed no mercy. After the leaders surrendered, they were quickly executed and their bodies thrown in quicklime behind a barrack's wall. The revulsion which swept Ireland at the cold-blooded executions was so intense that the hairs on the heads of the Irish did indeed "stand up." General Maxwell had not intended to stop the executions at sixteen—seventy-nine others had been condemned to death, but public outrage forced the English to grant a reprieve.[212] The circumstances of Connolly's execution particularly outraged public sensibility; he was so badly wounded that he had to be carried on a stretcher to the place of execution and was shot sitting on a chair. Yeats refers to this in his poem, "Three Songs to the One Burden": "Who was the first man shot that day? / The player Connolly, / Close to the City Hall he died; / Carriage and voice had he"(10–13). Elizabeth, Countess of Fingall, writes of the aftermath of the Rebellion:

> Then there were the slow executions, so many each morning. Sixteen in all. To the Irish people, being told of these executions in barracks yards, it was, as someone wrote "as though they watched a stream of blood coming from beneath a closed door."[213]

In spite of the terror, however, Pearse and his fellow poets faced their executions with "tragic joy" and unflinchingly played their parts. The following lines from "Lapiz Lazuli" could have been written for the 1916 poets, so heroic was their performance:

> All perform their tragic play,
> There struts Hamlet, there is Lear,
> That's Ophelia, that Cordelia;
> Yet they, should the last scene be there,
> The great stage curtain about to drop,
> If worthy their prominent part in the play,
> Do not break up their lines to weep.
> They know that Hamlet and Lear are gay;
> Gaiety transfiguring all that dread.
>
> (9–17)

The rebels, like great tragic actors, "do not break up their lines to weep." All of the leaders wrote cheerful letters to their families before their execution, and Pearse said of his impending execution: "This is the death I should have asked for if God had given me the choice of all deaths—to die a soldier's death for Ireland and for freedom."[214] Thus all the actors were "worthy their prominent part in the play."

In *The Decay of Lying*, which Oscar Wilde read to Yeats on Christmas Day 1888, Wilde maintained, "Life imitates art far more than Art imitates life. . . . A great artist invents a type, and life tries to copy it. . . ."[215] Yeats, in "The Trembling of the Veil," notes that Wilde read to him the following words from that essay on Christmas Day. "What does not the world owe to the imitation of Christ, what to the imitation of Caesar?"[216] Had Wilde lived to see the Easter Rebellion, he would perhaps have added, "What does not Ireland owe to the imitation of Cuchulain?" Irish literature and myth created for Pearse and his fellow poets, in the figure of Cuchulain, a "type" which they "consciously" imitated. Pearse, who was an avid reader of the *Tain*, tried to imitate not only Cuchulain's heroic courage but his heroic laughter.[217] and he spoke constantly of Cuchulain's defiant laughter when facing death:

Laughter is the crowning grace of the heroes. The epic tells how the dying Cuchulain noticed that a raven which had stopped to drink his blood, becoming entangled in the clotted gore, was ludicrously upset. Then Cuchulain, knowing that it was his last laugh, laughed aloud. I think that Emmet, I am quite sure that Tone, would have laughed in similar circumstances.[218]

Cuchulain's reckless laughter in the face of death was to Pearse characteristically Irish. In the June 1913 issue of *An Macaomh*, he wrote:

Here at St. Endas we have tried to keep before us the image of Fionn during his battles—careless and laughing, with that gesture of the head, that gallant smiling gesture, which has been an eternal gesture in Irish history; it was most memorably made by Emmet when he mounted the scaffold in Thomas Street. . . . I know that Ireland will not be happy again until she recollects that old proud gesture of hers, and that laughing gesture of a young man that is going into battle or climbing to a gibbet.[219]

In *The Green Helmet,* Yeats captures that "laughing gesture." The play is a heroic farce based on the saga *Bricrui's Feast* from the Ulster Cycle. In the play, the Red Man imposes upon the three greatest warriors of Ireland (Cuchulain, Conall and Laeghaire) a test to determine which one is the bravest. He tells them that they must prove their courage by allowing him to cut off their heads after they have cut off his. Cuchulain is the only one who will submit to this test, and when Emer pleads with him not to put his head to the axe, he replies:

> Little wife, little wife, be at rest.
> Alive I have been far off in all lands under
>   the sun
> And been no faithful man; but when my story
>   is done
> My fame shall spring up and laugh, and set
>   you high above all.[220]

It is uncanny that, as the Easter Rising drew near and Pearse, like Cuchulain, decided to lay his head upon the block, he writes a poem which seems to be a summary of the last speech given by the Red Man in Yeats's play. As the Red Man places the helmet of victory on Cuchulain, he declares:

> And I choose the laughing lip
> The heart that grows no bitterer though
>   betrayed by all;
> The hand that loves to scatter; the life like
>   a gambler's throw;
> And these things I make prosper, till a day
>   come that I know
> When heart and mind shall darken that the weak
>   may end the strong
> And the long-remembering harpers have matter
>   for their song.[221]

In Pearse's poem "The Fool," written just several months before his execution, Pearse writes that he is a "Fool that loved his folly." Like Cuchulain and the Red Man, who choose "the laughing lip" and "the hand that loves to scatter; the life like a gambler's throw," Pearse writes that he is "content to scatter the seed" and that as a "fool unrepentant" he shall at the end "laugh in his lonely heart as the ripe ears fall to the reaping hooks."[222]

So much did life imitate art during the Rebellion, that we are reminded of Yeats's observation, which I referred to in Chapter One, that "the elaborate technique of the arts . . . has taught more men to die than oratory or the Prayer Book." Pearse certainly used "the elaborate technique of the arts" to teach himself and others how to die, for his route to the firing squad was lined with his own dramatic presentations of heroic pageants based on the *Tain*. At the first anniversary of St. Endas, for example, Pearse produced his pageant *Mac-Ghniomharta Cuchulain* (The Boy-Deeds of Cuchulain), based on the story in the *Tain*. The play was a great success, and after the play Pearse addressed the crowds in the following words:

> We are anxious to crown our first year's work with something worthy and symbolic; anxious to send our boys home with the knightly image of Cuchulain in their hearts and his knightly words ringing in their ears. They will leave St. Endas under the spell of the magic of their most beloved hero.[223]

In the three years which preceded the Rebellion, Pearse organized many other heroic pageants based on the *Tain*, including the *Defence of the Ford*, which deals with the heroic stand made by Cuchulain and the Boy-Corps of Eamhain Macha against the enormous armies of Queen Maeve of Connacht—a scene which would be dramatically reenacted in 1916 when Pearse and a handful of his followers marched out (many of them armed with weapons which belonged in the ancient sagas)[224] to fight the armed might of the British Empire. Like Cuchulain, the men who fought in the General Post Office faced an army so enormous that it seemed like sheer madness to oppose it. Yet oppose it they did, and it is especially fitting that the Irish Government, in recognition of that fight against incredible odds, erected a statue of the dead Cuchulain in the General Post Office, the place where they made that heroic stand. It is also fitting that Yeats, who, perhaps more than anyone else, recognized the quest for beauty which lay at the back of the Rising, should at the end of his last play *The Death of Cuchulain*, leave us not with "polite meaningless words" about the Rebellion, but with the most beautiful Image of all—the sculptured body of Cuchulain: "No body like his body / Has modern woman born / . . . . A statue's there to mark the place, / By Oliver Sheppard done."[225] In *A Vision*, Yeats writes that "all unity is from the Mask . . . and the self so sought is that Unity of Being compared by Dante in the *Convito* to that of 'a perfectly proportioned human body.'"[226] The "perfectly proportioned" body of Cuchulain, frozen forever into the fierce geometry of stone, "embodies" the "terrible beauty" of the Rebellion in a way no words ever could. As an ancient talisman of perfect form standing defiantly against the "formlessness" of modern life, it is a constant reminder to the modern Irish that, although Ireland is a country which has been "maimed" with "great hatred" and a "fanatic heart," it is also a country capable of the grandest heroism and the greatest art:

> We Irish, born into that ancient sect
> But thrown upon this filthy modern tide
> And by its formless spawning fury wrecked
> Climb to our proper dark, that we may trace
> The lineaments of a plummet-measured face.
>
> ("The Statues," 27–32)

The "proper dark" that Yeats mentions here suggests the rich ancestral darkness of the great tapestry, which, according to Yeats, still colors the modern Irish imagination. For a time, however, Yeats felt that the links with that ancient tapestry had been broken. In 1907, fearing that the romantic nationalism so vividly portrayed in the designs of that tapestry was dying, Yeats wrote:

> Poetical tragedy, and indeed all the more intense forms of literature, had lost their hold on the general mass of men in other countries as life grew safe. . . . but I believed that the memory of danger, and the reality of it seemed near enough sometimes, would last long enough to give Ireland her imaginative opportunity. I could not foresee that a new class, which had begun to rise into power under the shadow of Parnell, would change the nature of the Irish movement, which, needing no longer great sacrifice, nor bringing any great risk to individuals, could do without exceptional men, and those activities of the mind that are founded on the exceptional moment. . . . Ireland's great moment had passed, and she had filled no roomy vessels with strong sweet wine. . . .[227]

Yeats, of course, was wrong, and the poetic and nationalistic explosion of the Easter Rising nine years later showed him how wrong. The Rebellion proved that "poetical tragedy" had not lost its hold on the Irish imagination, that Ireland's "great moment" had not passed, and that "great sacrifices" were not a thing of the past. The Rebellion also proved that the Mask and the dramatic gesture, which Pearse described as an "eternal gesture in Irish history," were still potent forces in Irish life. Yeats had also written in 1907 that "artists are the servants of life in its nobler forms, where joy and sorrow are one, Artificers of the Great Moment."[228] When Yeats found himself in 1916 the "Artificer" of the "Great Moment," he turned to the very symbol of artifice itself—the Mask—as a form through which he wished to convey the spirit of the Rebellion. And the "players" in the great drama provided Ireland with her "imaginative opportunity." They faced the British firing squads "like Shakespeare's persons, who, when the last darkness has gathered about them, speak out of an ecstasy that is one-half the surrender of sorrow, and one-half the last playing and mockery of the victorious sword before the defeated world."[229] The Mask, as Yeats has written, is always "a Work of Art."[230]

3

The Kiss of Death

Red Rose, proud Rose, sad Rose of all my days!
Come near me, while I sing the ancient ways:
Cuchulain battling with the bitter tide;
The Druid, grey, wood-nutured, quiet-eyed,
Who cast round Fergus dreams, and ruin untold;
And thine own sadness, where of stars, grown old
In dancing silver-sandalled on the sea,
Sing in their high and lonely melody.
Come near, that no more blinded by man's fate,
I find under the boughs of love and hate,
In all poor foolish things that live a day,
Eternal beauty wandering on her way.

W. B. Yeats, "The Rose"

O N 2 April 1916, while Pearse and the other members of the "cult of Cuchulain" were preparing themselves spiritually for the symbolic Masks which they would don in the Easter Rebellion, Yeats was rehearsing with real Masks a play *(At the Hawk's Well)* which had for its theme the initiation of the warrior Cuchulain into a life of tragic beauty and heroism. The quest for beauty, which lay at the back of the Rising and which pervades the poetry, plays, and essays of the 1916 poets, informs *At the Hawk's Well* and the four other plays which make up the Cuchulain play cycle—*The Green Helmet, On Baile's Strand, The Only Jealousy of Emer,* and *The Death of Cuchulain.* The plays are structured around the conflict between two opposing worlds— the world of "terrible beauty" that accompanies the heroic Mask and the comfortable world of home and hearth that both Cuchulain and the poets of 1916 reject in favor of the heroic life. And just as the Black Rose cast her fatal shadow over both the lives of the 1916 poets and the landscape of their poetry, so too the Woman of the Sidhe (highly suggestive of Ireland in one of her seductive Masks) lures Cuchulain to his death in the Cuchulain play cycle. Although critics in their interpretation of the Cuchulain plays have commented on the importance of the Sidhe as agents of the heroic Mask, they have overlooked the important connection between the Woman of the Sidhe and Ireland herself. In Chapters 1 and 2, I discussed how it was the hypnotic beauty of Ireland herself, personified through her poetic Mask as a woman, that compelled generation after generation of young Irish men to don the heroic Mask: "Praise God if this my blood fulfills the doom / When you dark rose, shall redden into bloom."[1] And I believe that Yeats in the Cuchulain plays intended the Sidhe, at least on one level,[2] to stand for the fatal beauty of Ireland herself. In short, Yeats saw the surrender of Cuchulain to the Sidhe as symbolic of the surrender, throughout Irish history, of countless poet patriots to the Goddess Ireland, who, generation after generation, as Heaney points out, "swallows our love and our terror."[3] John Rees Moore, commenting on the significance of the Sidhe in the Cuchulain plays, writes that the Woman of the Sidhe "represents a challenge to battle that combines a kind of religious commitment with sexual ardour."[4] As already noted, Ireland herself historically evoked just such a response in her patriots—a response where erotic desire and spiritual devotion were strangely linked. In Chapter 1, we have seen this powerful combination in the erotic death poems of the rebels dedicated to the Black Rose, and in the Cuchulain plays the Black Rose and the Woman of the Sidhe have much in common. They are, in fact, different facets of the same seductive Mask that traces its lineaments back to the great Irish tapestry. The "terrible beauty" of this Mask evokes in those who behold it a desire to sacrifice themselves by seeking their own heroic Mask and the elusive beauty that only death can bring. Yeats, referring to Red Hanrahan in "The Twisting of the Rope," writes of the dilemma that afflicts those who have been called by such women:

> It is a pity for him that refuses the call of the daughters of the Sidhe, for he will find no comfort in the love of the women of the earth to the end of life and time, and the cold of the grave is in his heart for ever. It is death he has chosen; let him die, let him die, let him die.[5]

And in his descriptions of the various dynasties of Irish fairies which appeared in *Lucifer*, Yeats writes of the tragic fate of the victims of the Leanhaun Shee (fairy mistress) who, like the Black Rose, seeks the love of men:

> Her lovers waste away, for she lives on their life. Most of the Gaelic poets, down to quite recent times, have had a Leanhaun Shee, for she gives inspiration to her slaves. She is the Gaelic muse. . . . Her lovers, the Gaelic poets, died young. She grew restless, and carried them away to other worlds, for death does not destroy her power.[6]

For Irish poets, of course, Ireland herself has been the greatest muse, and the Leanhaun Shee is but one of her many Masks. MacDonagh, for example, refers alternately to both the Woman of the Sidhe and to Ireland herself as the Gaelic muse who inspired his poetry. In his poem "Fairy Tales," for example, he writes:

> O spirits heaven born!
> O kind De Danann souls,
> Whose music down our story rolls,
> And holds it near the morn,
>
> You stir the poet heart
> To dream in quickening rimes
> The magic of the fairy times
> That never shall depart![7]

In his poem "Inscriptions of Ireland," on the other hand, he identifies Ireland herself as the Gaelic Muse:

> My poet years and shudders with desire
> To bring to speech your music's intense thought:
> It is music all, yet he in ice and fire
> Excruciates till it to words is wrought.[8]

The lovers of Ireland, like the lovers of the Leanhaun Shee, "die young" for "she lives on their lives": "For Patrick Pearse had said / That in every generation / Must Ireland's blood be shed."[9] Certainly MacDonagh, Pearse and Plunkett—three "Gaelic poets" who referred to themselves in their poetry as "lovers" of Ireland—followed in the footsteps of former lovers of the Leanhaun Shee and, sacrificing themselves upon the altar of their muse, "died young." In the Cuchulain play cycle, Cuchulain, like the 1916 poets, is afflicted by the call of the Sidhe, and the cycle can be seen as an illumination of the conflict which faces all those devotees of the Black Rose who choose the heroic Mask over the values of the hearth. Furthermore, if we look first at the literary works of the 1916 poets and then at the individual plays in the Cuchulain play cycle, we shall see that both focus on this conflict.

The "dark way" of ecstasy and heroic transcendance chosen by Cuchulain in Yeats's play cycle and by the followers of the "dark Rose" throughout Irish history is mentioned by Plunkett in his poem "The Dark Way":

> Rougher than Death the road I choose
> Yet shall my feet not walk astray,
> Though dark, my way I shall not lose
> For this way is the darkest way.[10]

By choosing the "darkest way," Plunkett must reject the comfortable life of the hearth he could have shared with his fiancee Grace Gifford: "No more shall I share ease / No more shall I spare blood / . . . Now I shall seek to die."[11] In his poem "Heaven in Hell" he writes about his decision to adopt the heroic Mask:

> I chose, and joined the band
> Of Heaven's adventurers that seek

> To climb the never-conquered peak
> In solitude by their sole might.[12]

MacDonagh, like Plunkett, seeks to "climb the never-conquered peak" and, like Major Robert Gregory, to experience "that lonely impulse of delight."[13] In his poem "John-John" he has the wife of such an individual say to her husband "You know you never were the stuff / To be the cottage cat / To watch the fire and hear me lock / The door and put out Shep."[14] And in his poem "Envoi," referring to the "dark way" he has chosen, he declares: "But I whose creed is only death / Do not prize their victory / I know that my life is but a breath / On the glass of eternity."[15]

Pearse, like MacDonagh and Plunkett, was very much drawn to the comforts of the hearth which he was forced to renounce in order to don the heroic Mask. His two plays *The Singer* and *The Master* contrast the solitary life of the hero with the comfortable life of the hearth. In *The Singer*, MacDara, a poet very much like Pearse, realizes that, if he is to save Ireland, he must do more than write poetry—he must don the Antithetical Mask of the warrior:

> I have done nothing all my life but think; think and make poems. . . . Can the Vision beautiful alone content a man? I think true man is divine in this, that, like God, he must needs create, he must needs do.[16]

Once he has chosen his Mask, once he has done this "hard, sweet thing,"[17] MacDara, like Pearse, enters wholeheartedly into his role as warrior: "One man can free a people as one man redeemed the world. I will take no pike, I will go into the battle with bare hands."[18]

Yet for MacDara as for Pearse, the attraction of the hearth always remains, and throughout the play Pearse returns again and again to the image of the fireplace where MacDara's mother and sweetheart sit:

> MACDARA: Mother, sometimes when I was in the middle of great crowds, I have seen this fireplace, and you standing with your hands stretched out to me as you stood a minute ago, and Sighle in the doorway of the room, and my heart has cried out to you.[19]

At the end of the play as MacDara rushes out to meet his death, the audience is allowed to catch a glimpse, for the last time, of the world that MacDara has been forced to renounce in order to save Ireland. Just before the curtain descends we see MacDara's mother and sweetheart sitting once again by the fire—the symbol of the warmth and security to which Pearse himself was drawn.

In Pearse's play *The Master*, the world of the hearth is again contrasted to the world of vision and heroic sacrifice. Ciaran, sounding very much like Pearse himself, declares:

This is a hard thing that I found to do, to live lonely and unbeloved among my own kin. Daire has not done anything as hard as this. In one of the cities that I had sailed to I had heard of the true, illustrious God, and of men who had gone out from warm and pleasant houses, and from the kindly faces of neighbours to live in desert places, where God walked alone and terrible; and I said that I would do that hard thing, though I would fain have stayed in my father's house. . . .[20]

Pearse, like Ciaran, had to struggle hard with himself and his natural desire to stay amid the "warm and pleasant houses" of Ireland, for the road of the revolutionary poet is a lonely one and the road to the firing squad even lonelier. This intense conflict with one's Antithetical Mask is what creates the hero. As Leonard Nathan in *The Tragic Drama of William Butler Yeats* points out, unlike the saint who attains perfection by rejecting the world, the hero reaches perfection by his ability to both embrace and yet transcend the very world he loves.[21] Nathan observes that the process of "conflict, defeat, superhuman vision, and Unity of Being, is for Yeats, tragic,"[22] both in the sense that it involves the loss of the world with its beauties and pleasures and in the sense that the process converts that loss into a state of being far superior to the "anima hominis" at its best. In Pearse's play, King Daire, who represents the world of practical wisdom as opposed to the world of "super-human vision," scoffs at those who embark on the heroic quest, and accuses Ciaran of wasting his life chasing shadows:

> KING DAIRE: You seem to me to have spent your life pursuing shadows
>   that fled before you; yea, pursuing ghosts over wide spaces
>   and through the devious places of the world: and I pity you
>   for the noble manhood you have wasted. I seem to you to
>   have spent my life busy with the little, vulgar tasks and the
>   little, vulgar pleasures of a King: and you pity me because I
>   have not adventured, because I have not suffered as you
>   have. . . .[23]

The conflict between the world of the hearth and the world of heroic beauty that we see in *The Master* and *The Singer* appears again in Yeats's play *At the Hawk's Well*. The old man in the play, like the king in Pearse's drama, speaks of a life spent "pursuing shadows that fled":

> The accursed shadows have deluded me,
> The stones are dark and yet the well is empty;
> The water flowed and emptied while I slept.
> You have deluded me my whole life through,
> Accursed dancers, you have stolen my life,
> That there should be such evil in a shadow.[24]

The shadow, the old man declares, is "the Woman of the Sidhe herself / The mountain witch, the unappeasable shadow / She is always flitting upon this mountain-side, / To allure or to destroy."[25] In the play she appears in the form of a hawk, takes possession of the guardian of the well, and through her dance arouses Cuchulain to desire and madness. Cuchulain, like the poets of 1916, is highly susceptible to such beauty. This is underlined in the old man's words to Cuchulain: "What mischief brings you hither? You are like those who are crazy for the shedding of men's blood, and for the love of women."[26] Love and death are linked together in this phrase as they are in the poems of the 1916 poets and in the entire Cuchulain play cycle. And the woman of the Sidhe, as described in *At the Hawk's Well*, has all the fatal attributes of the Black Rose herself. She is linked throughout the play, for example, with the image of the stone, which was a central metaphor in "Easter 1916," and, as noted earlier, the stone obviously symbolizes the fatal beauty of Inisfail herself. In the play, the Sidhe are described as those who "dance among the stones."[27] The guardian of the well, who is possessed by the Woman of the Sidhe, is described as having eyes that "know nothing, or but look upon stone."[28] She is like the rebels in "Easter 1916" who are possessed by the Black Rose and, as a result, have "hearts enchanted to a stone." Even Cuchulain's death in the play cycle is linked with his desire for a goddess whose fierce beauty is associated with stone. It is "rock-nurtured Aoife,"[29] the warrior queen of the "stone-pale cheek,"[30] who arouses in Cuchulain the desire for sexual conquest and who eventually leads him to his death. At the end of *At the Hawk's Well*, we are told that Cuchulain rushes out after the Hawk Woman (Aoife's accomplice), "shouldering his spear and calling 'He comes, Cuchulain, son of Sualtim, comes.'"[31] The spear here has strong phallic implications (as it has in the *Tain* and in the poems of the 1916 poets),[32] for we know that Cuchulain, "that violent amorous man"[33] seized by his desire for battle and sexual conquest will soon master Aoife, and their violent sexual union will seal his doom. In *On Baile's Strand*, Aoife is prophetically linked with a "pillar-stone" similar to the one upon which Cuchulain will later die":

> There was a boy in her house that had her own red colour on him and everybody said he was to be brought up to kill Cuchulain, that she hated Cuchulain. She used to put a helmet on a pillar-stone and call it Cuchulain and set him casting at it.[34]

Finally, in the last play of the cycle, *The Death of Cuchulain*, the stone emerges as a central metaphor which binds all of the plays in the cycle together. Yeats's masterful use of the stone image in this final play convinces me that in the entire play cycle he intended the Woman of the Sidhe and the other warrior goddesses of fierce stonelike beauty to stand for the fatal beauty of Inisfail herself. At the end of the play, the wounded Cuchulain ties himself to a "pillar-stone" in order to meet death on his feet: "I have put my belt / About this stone and want to fasten it / And die upon my feet. . . ."[35] Significantly, it is Aoife who presides over this ceremony of death. In a gesture which seems to symbolize their past sexual union, she winds her veil about the pillar-stone so that he may not escape: ". . . and that your strength may not start up when the time comes / I wind my veil about this ancient stone."[36] Aiofe's description of the stone as "ancient" is also significant, for it suggests that the stone has connections with Lia Fail, the ancient Stone of Destiny, and therefore, by extension, with Inisfail herself. Furthermore, for Cuchulain, the pillar-stone actually is his "Stone of Destiny" because it is tied to this stone that he meets his death and fulfills his heroic destiny, just as the 1916 poets fulfilled their destiny dying for Inisfail. As he appears to have done in "Easter 1916," Yeats once again, in the Cuchulain play cycle, masterfully uses the image of the stone to suggest both the enchanted and the fatal qualities of Ireland herself.

Yeats's frequent use of the stone symbol throughout the play cycle suggests that he was consciously attempting to unify his plays around a single metaphor. Most of the plays in the cycle are based on the Japanese Noh form, and Yeats admired the Noh for what he saw as "a playing upon a single metaphor, as deliberate as the echoing rhythm of line in Chinese and Japanese painting."[37] He writes that, in the Noh play *Nishikigi*, "the ghost of the girl-lover carrier the cloth she went on weaving out of grass when she should have opened the chamber door to her lover, and woven grass returns again and again in metaphor and incident. . . ."[38] In *Hagoromo*, Yeats notes, "the feather mantle of the faery woman creates also its rhythm of metaphor."[39] Just as the feather mantle of the "faery woman" in *Hagoromo* unifies the whole play, so too the enchanted stone, symbol of Ireland and the Women of the Sidhe who hover around it, binds all of the Cuchulain plays together.

In *At the Hawk's Well*, the first play in the Cuchulain play cycle, Yeats connects the dreaming wisdom of the Sidhe with the stones in the well. He identifies the Sidhe in this play as the enemies of the hearth, and they remain such throughout the entire play cycle:

> The man that I praise
> Lives all his days
> Where a hand on the bell
> Can call the milch cows
> To the comfortable door of his house,
> Who but an idiot would praise
> Dry stones in a well?
>
> The man that I praise
> Has married and stays
> By an old hearth, and he
> On naught has set store
> But children and dogs on the floor.[40]

In the plays, the Sidhe act as those "personifying spirits" which Yeats in his doctrine of the Mask describes as "Gates and Gatekeepers, because through their dramatic power they bring our souls to crisis, to Mask and Image."[41] As Helen Vendler point out in *Yeats's Vision and the Later Plays*, it is the Woman of the Sidhe who leads Cuchulain away from longevity and a life of ease toward the conflict which will allow him to fulfill his heroic fate. Thus, Vendler concludes, the Hawk-woman can be seen in some sense as his "Daimon, a Muse of battle."[42] Yeats's descriptions of the Daimon in "Per Amica Silentia Lunae" further illuminate the role of the Sidhe as agents of the heroic Mask:

> I think that all religious men have believed that there is a hand not ours in the events of life, and that, as somebody says in Wilhelm Meister, accident is destiny; and I think it was Heraclitus who said: the Daimon is our destiny. When I think of life as a struggle with the Daimon who would ever set us to the hardest work among those not impossible, I understand why there is a deep enmity between a man and his destiny, and why a man loves nothing but his destiny. In an Anglo-Saxon poem a certain man is called, as though to call him something that summed up all heroism, "Doom eager."[43]

Plunkett, one of those "doom eager"[44] young men like Cuchulain, in his description of the Sidhe as "dreamers of doom," in "White Waves on the Water," accurately defines the role they play as weavers of the heroic Mask in Yeats's plays. In the plays, the Sidhe, like Yeats's "Daimon," "bring man again and again to the place of choice, heightening temptation that the choice may be as final as possible."[45] As Nathan points out, although it is Cuchulain himself who freely "chooses" to accept his heroic fate, it is the Goddess or "daemonic power" who confronted him with that choice.[46]

Again and again throughout the play cycle, Cuchulain is confronted with the choice between the values of the hearth, represented by human women like Emer, and the heroic life, represented by the Women of the Sidhe. In *The Green Helmet*, for example, Cuchulain, because of his decision to lay his head beneath the Red Man's Axe, risks losing all of the joys of the hearth, which are represented in the play by Emer. Emer pleads with Cuchulain to stay home, but he tells her, "You are young, you are wise, you can call some kinder and comelier man that will sit home in the house."[47] In the following lines which Cuchulain speaks to Emer at the end of the play, he asks her to recognize his heroic nature and not to interfere with his chosen fate: "Would you stay the great barnacle-goose / When its eyes are turned to the sea and its beak to the salt of the air?"[48]

In *On Baile's Strand* Cuchulain again fights hard to maintain his heroic identity and his alliance with the Sidhe against Conchubar, who wishes to domesticate him. Conchubar, we are told, wants Cuchulain to take an oath of obedience which will "make him biddable as a house-dog and keep him always at his hand."[49] Conchubar's children, who are themselves timid creatures of the hearth, are afraid of Cuchulain's wild heroic nature and beg their father to control him: "How can we be at safety with this man / That nobody can buy or bid or bind? / We shall be at his mercy when you are gone / He burns the earth as if he were a fire. . . ."[50] Cuchulain's passion, like the passion of the Sidhe, is a pure flame that consumes all those exposed to it. Pearse, like Yeats, greatly admired such passion and sees it in the patriots whose Masks he most revered. Two years before the Rising, Pearse wrote of Parnell that he was less a political thinker than an "embodied conviction; a flame that seared, a sword that stabbed."[51] In men like Cuchulain and all the great Irish heroes, including the ancient Fenians and their modern counterparts, Pearse sees this same searing passion. In words which seem to forecast the Easter Rebellion, he speaks of his belief that such passion will purify Ireland:

> By the Fenian spirit I mean not so much the spirit of a particular generation as that virile fighting faith which has been the salt of all the generations of Ireland unto the last. And is it here even in this last? Yea, its seeds are here, and behold they are kindling: it is for you and me to fan them into such a flame as shall consume everything that is mean and compromising and insincere in Ireland. . . . When we stand armed as Volunteers we shall at least be men, and shall be able to come into communion of thought and action with the virile generations of Ireland.[52]

In Yeats's story "Hanrahan and Cathleen" Hanrahan, a member of the "virile generations of Ireland" tells us that such flaming passions are passed on directly by Ireland herself in one of her exquisite Masks—Cathleen Ni Houlihan:

> The old brown thorn-trees break in two high
> over Cummen Strand,
> Under a bitter black wind that blows from
> the left hand;
> Our courage breaks like an old tree in a
> black wind and dies,
> But we have hidden in our hearts the flame
> out of the eyes
> Of Cathleen, the daughter of Houlihan.[53]

Over the centuries, the "virile generations" of Ireland with the "flame out of the eyes of Cathleen" in their hearts have left home and hearth to defend her. So too Cuchulain, the most virile of all Irish warriors, succumbs to the seductive beauty of Cathleen's spirit counterparts—the Women of the Sidhe.

In *On Baile's Strand*, Conchubar tries to break the bond of passion which links Cuchulain with the Sidhe and by extension with his heroic Mask, by forcing Cuchulain to take an oath of obedience that will chain him to the hearth. Since the Sidhe are the enemies of "the threshold and the hearthstone"[54] Conchubar uses fire from the hearth to exorcize the power of the Sidhe:

> May this fire have driven out
> The Shape-Changers that can put
> Ruin on a great kings' house
> Until all be ruinous.
> Names whereby a man has known
> The threshold and the hearthstone
> Gather on the wind and drive
> The women none can kiss and thrive,
> For they are but whirling wind,
> Out of memory and mind.
> They would make a prince decay
>
> .   .   .   .
>
> For many shapes they have,
> They would change them into hounds,
>
> .   .   .   .
>
> Or they hurl a spell at him,
> That he follow with desire
> Bodies that can never tire.[55]

The Women of the Sidhe—those "women none can kiss and thrive"—bestow upon their victims great ecstasy and great beauty, but at the cost of human life. Like the kiss of death planted upon the lips of her devotees by the Black Rose, the kiss of the Woman of the Sidhe plants in the hearts of her victims a desire which no human woman can ever satisfy. Pearse was certainly one marked by such a kiss of death, and in his poem "Why do you Torture Me" he reveals his awareness that only in death will he experience the consummation of his love for the Black Rose:

> Why are you torturing me, O desires of my heart?
> Torturing me and paining me by day and by night?
> Hunting me as a poor deer would be hunted on a
>   hill,
> A poor long-wearied deer with the hound-pack
>   after him?
> There's no ease to my paining in the loneliness
>   of the hills,
> But the cry of the hunters terrifically to be
>   heard,
> The cry of my desires haunting me without
>   respite,
> O ravening hounds, long is your run!

No satisfying can come to my desires while I
    live,
For the satisfaction I desired yesterday is no
    satisfaction,
And the hound-pack is the greedier of the
    satisfaction it has got
And forever I shall not sleep till I sleep in
    the grave.[56]

Pearse, like Yeats in *On Baile's Strand,* uses the image of the hounds to reflect unquenchable desire. In doing so, Pearse it sticking close to the symbolic language of Irish mythology. Yeats, in the notes to his poem "The Wanderings of Oisin," writes that in Irish mythology the image of the hound often represents the sexual desire of man for woman, And in "Red Hanrahan" the hounds of the Sidhe are used by Yeats in exactly this way. Hanrahan is lured by the hounds away from his human sweetheart Mary Lavelle to Slieve Echtge where he is hypnotized by the beauty of Echtge—a woman of the Sidhe. Echtge clearly represents Ireland herself, for, as mentioned earlier, her symbol in the story is the Stone of Destiny.

Over and over again in his writings, Pearse stresses the need for Irish men to assert their virility by taking up arms in defense of the Black Rose: "When the young men of a nation have reached so terrible a depth as to be unconscious of the dignity of arms, one will naturally doubt their capacity for any virile thought, let alone any virile action."[57] Since virile thought and virile action are bound up with Cuchulain's allegiance to the Sidhe in Yeats's plays, Conchubar's attempts to draw Cuchulain away from the Sidhe can be seen as an attempt to reduce that virility and to diminish Cuchulain's heroic stature. Conchubar is far more dangerous to Cuchulain than the Sidhe, for, although the Sidhe lead Cuchulain to battle and to death, they do not cause him to betray his heroic nature, but rather to fulfill it. Conchubar, on the other hand, by forcing Cuchulain to thrust his sword blade in the fire to renounce the Sidhe, forces him to renounce his deepest self:

Therefore in this ancient cup
May the sword-blades drink their fill
Of the home-brew there, until
They will have for masters none
But the threshold and hearthstone.[58]

But, as the play reveals, Cuchulain is not one who is comfortable with the "home-brew," and the servile Mask Conchubar would have Cuchulain wear is a "False Mask." As Bloom points out in his analysis of the Cuchulain plays, Cuchulain's True Mask is, according to phase twelve, Self-exaggeration, and his False Mask—Self-abandonment.[59] The awakening of the "antithetical being" of the hero, Yeats writes in phase twelve of *A Vision,* produces a "noble extravagance, an overflowing fountain of personal life."[60] It is this "noble extravagance" this "overflowing fountain of personal life" that Conchubar forces Cuchulain momentarily to renounce in favor of the False Mask of Self-abandonment. The result for Cuchulain, in *On Baile's Strand*, is madness. Having betrayed the Sidhe (his natural kin according to Vendler) and, as a result, himself, he ends up killing his own son. At the end of the play, however, Cuchulain realizes that he has been tricked by Conchubar and that it is because of Conchubar, who forced upon him a False Mask, that his son is dead. Although he has been blaming the Sidhe for the killing of his son, he suddenly realizes that the Sidhe have never been interested in such futile destructive violence:

> But no, for they have always been my friends;
> And though they love to blow a smoking coal
> Till it's all flame, the wars they blow aflame
> Are full of glory, and heart-uplifting pride,
> And not like this. The wars they love awaken
> Old fingers and the sleepy string of harps.[61]

In these lines, Yeats explicitly identifies the Sidhe as agents of the heroic Mask, both on an individual and a national level. They lead not only individuals to their True Mask but nations as well: ". . . the wars they blow aflame / Are full of glory." They are like "gatekeepers who drive the nation to war or anarchy that it may find its Image . . ."[62] or True Mask. Thus, Ireland, in the passion and heroism of the Easter Rising found its True Mask, and "the sleepy strings of harps" once again, as in the old sagas, "awakened to its glory." Had Pearse, MacDonagh and Plunkett succumbed to the comforts of the "hearth," had the call of the Black Rose been less powerful, her beauty less consuming, the Easter Rising would never have taken place. But, like Cuchulain, who could not resist the beauty of the Sidhe and followed them to his doom, the 1916 poets were totally devoted to the Black Rose. MacDonagh, in his poem to the poet James Clarence Mangan, praises Mangan for the same singular devotion to the Black Rose that led MacDonagh himself to the firing squad: ". . . Though to thy hand / All strings of music throbbed, thy single love / Was, in high trust, to hymn thy Gaelic land / And passionate proud woes of Roisin Dubh [Black Rose]."[63]

The Sidhe, like the Black Rose, represent the call of erotic desire, of art, and of death—the lineaments from which Ireland's poetic Mask, over the centuries, has been traced. Thus, in the work of Yeats and the 1916 poets, the Sidhe and the Black Rose represent different facets of the same poetic Mask—the Mask of Ireland herself. Furthermore, if we see the Woman of the Sidhe as representing an aspect of Ireland herself, then the critical arguments regarding what Fand, the Woman of the Sidhe, represents in *The Only Jealousy of Emer*, are resolved. Peter Ure, for example, sees Fand as a symbol of death: "The mythological theme is used to present a strange drama of conflict—a conflict between human love and the abstraction of death, between Emer and the Woman of the Sidhe. . . ."[64] Vendler, on the other hand, disagrees with Ure's perception of Fand as a symbol of death and sees her instead as a symbol of aesthetic perfection.[65] Reg Skene and F. A. C. Wilson see Fand as representing erotic desire, and Bloom partially agrees with this theory, stating that the strength of the play results from its "coherence and insight in handling Yeats's most difficult theme, the genesis of love and beauty in phases 14 and 15."[66] He emphatically rejects, however, Vendler's belief that Fand represents the poetic Muse, stating that "we need to remember that the hero is not the poet, and so his relations with the Sidhe are not the poet's relations with the Muse."[67] In Ireland, however, the hero is often the poet. As discussed earlier, Cuchulain as the *Tain's* most splendid warrior poet remains one of the most potent icons of Irish nationality.

As I have already suggested, all of the critical arguments about what Fand represents are resolved if we consider Fand as symbolizing an aspect of Ireland herself. Ireland served throughout Irish history as Poetic Muse, Seductive Mistress, and Goddess of Death for her followers. And Fand, in *The Only Jealousy of Emer,* can be seen to represent all of these, rather than any one alone. Given Yeats's love of traditional Irish symbols such as the stone, with rich and complex levels of meaning, this conclusion is, I believe, the most valid. Certainly the beauty of Fand, like the beauty of Ireland herself, outshines all human beauty. Cuchulain equates her beauty with the perfect beauty of phase fifteen:

> Who is it stands before me there
> Shedding such light from limb and hair
> As when the moon, complete at last
> With every labouring crescent past,
> And lonely with extreme delight,
> Flings out upon the fifteenth night?[68]

And Fand, like Ireland, is lonely in that beauty. She awaits, like Echtge ("Ireland"), in "Red Hanrahan," a human lover to awaken her, and promises Cuchulain ecstasy if he will grant her a kiss:

> Because I long I am not complete. . . .
> Time shall seem to stay his course;
> When your mouth and my mouth meet
> All my round shall be complete
> Imagining all its circles run;
> And there shall be oblivion
> Even to quench Cuchulain's drouth,
> Even to still that heart.[69]

Fand, although beautiful, requires the sacrifice of her lovers to make her complete, just as Yeats's Rose Tree requires the sacrificial blood of the rebels to make it bloom. In the play, Fand's elaborate beauty stands opposed to the human beauty of Emer and Eithne. Emer, and Eithne in a lesser way, represent the values of the hearth as opposed to the values of the heroic life represented by Fand, and, as in the other plays in the cycle, these two modes of existence are contrasted throughout the play: "But all the enchantments of the dreaming foam / Dread the hearth fire."[70] Fand, who has risen out of the "dreaming foam," seeks out men with poetic souls for her lovers because she knows they will be most vulnerable to her beauty:

> She has hurried from the Country-under-Wave
> And dreamed herself into that shape that he
> May glitter in her basket for the Sidhe
> Are dexterous fishers and they fish for
> Men with dreams upon the hook.[71]

Pearse, Plunkett and MacDonagh were "men with dreams upon the hook"— "We know their dream; enough / To know they dreamed and are dead. . . ." Emer, referring to the inhuman beauty of the Sidhe, with which human women find it impossible to compete, declares:

> They find our men asleep . . .
> Lap them in cloudy hair or kiss their lips
> Our men awake in ignorance of it all
> But when we take them in our arms at night
> We cannot break their solitude . . .[72]

Certainly, the human wives and sweethearts of the 1916 rebels, like Emer and Eithne, found it difficult to compete with the inhuman beauty of Cathleen Ni Houlihan and in the end could not save them from her fatal embrace. One can only imagine the helplessness felt by Grace Gifford when her husband of several minutes (Plunkett) was led directly from their wedding to his execution, just as Michael in *Cathleen Ni Houlihan* was stolen by Cathleen from Delia on the eve of her wedding. Like Grace, Muriel (MacDonagh's wife) suffered greatly by her husband's death. MacDonagh was happily married with two children when he was executed, and just three years before the Rising he had written of his great love for his family in a poem to his son entitled "Wishes for My Son":

> Now, my son, is life for you,
> And I wish you joy of it,
> Joy of power in all you do,
> Deeper passion, better wit
> Than I who had enough,
> Quicker life and length thereof,
> More of every gift but love.

Love I have beyond all men,
Love that now you share with me
What have I to wish you then
But that you be good and free,
And that God to you may give
Grace in stronger days to live?[33]

Yet this man who had "love beyond all men" responded to the call of the
Black Rose, sacrificing all that human love could offer. MacDonagh's wife
Muriel was devastated by his death. Norstedt, in his biography of Mac-
Donagh, points out that Muriel, who suffered from nervous disorders, was
emotionally dependent upon her husband and that when he died she felt
totally lost. Within one year she herself was dead—drowned while swimming
to an offshore island from Skerries.[74] Although Pearse was not married, he
was totally devoted to his mother and sisters and, like Plunkett and Mac-
Donagh, was willing to give up all that he loved in order to set the Black Rose
free. Although one of Pearse's sisters begged him not to go through with his
plans for the Rising, which she saw as suicidal, Pearse's determination to
sacrifice himself for Ireland could not be broken. In his poem "The Fool,"
written several months before the Rebellion, he answers those who accuse
him of being a dreamer and a fool and defends the dream out of which the
Rising was born:

The lawyers have sat in council, the men with
    the keen long faces,
And said, "This man is a fool," and others
    have said, "He blasphemeth";
And the wise have pitied the fool that hath
    striven to give a life
In the world of time and space among the bulks
    of actual things
To a dream that was dreamed in the heart, and
    that only the heart could hold.

O wise men riddle me this: what if the dream
    come true?
What if the dream come true? And if millions
    unborn shall dwell
In the house that I shaped in my heart, the
    noble house of my thought?
Lord I have staked my soul, I have staked
    the lives of my kin
On the truth of thy dreadful word. Do not
    remember my failures
But remember this my faith. . . .[75]

Pearse and all the other followers of the Black Rose who over the centuries
have built in the "noble house" of their thoughts an imperishable image of

the Goddess Ireland that transcends all human beauty do not waver in their devotion. In *The Only Jealousy of Emer*, the figure of Cuchulain reminds Emer of the difficulty that human women face in attempting to draw their men away from such an icon: "You've watched his loves and / You had not been jealous / Knowing he would tire, but do those tire / That love the Sidhe?"[76] Yeats's stage directions regarding Fand's Mask and his comments in his notes to the play clearly connect her with the most noble of all icons—Ireland herself. Yeats writes that Fand's "Mask and clothes must suggest gold or bronze . . . so that she seems more an idol than a human being."[77] And in his notes he describes the woman of the Sidhe in her stylized gold Mask as a "strange, noble, unforgettable figure,"[78]—adjectives which are applicable to Cathleen Ni Houlihan, Countess Cathleen, Echtge, and his other person-ifications of Ireland. Furthermore, in his poem, "The Secret Rose," Yeats links Fand not only with the spiritual beauty of the Alchemical Rose but with the Black Rose herself and the kiss of death she bestows:

> Far-off, most secret, and inviolate Rose,
> Enfold me in my hour of hours; where those
> Who sought thee in the Holy Sepulchre,
> Or in the wine-vat, dwell beyond the stir
> And tumult of defeated dreams;
>
> .   .   .   .
>
> . . . and him
> Who met Fand walking among flaming dew
> By a grey shore where the wind never blew,
> And lost the world and Emer for a kiss.[79]

Such a kiss, Fand promises Cuchulain in the play, will wipe out all human attachments and all human memories, so that only beauty will remain: "Then kiss my mouth. Though memory / Be beauty's bitterest enemy / I have no dread, for at my kiss / Memory on the moment vanishes / Nothing but beauty can remain." Although Cuchulain in *The Only Jealousy of Emer* is, at the last minute, snatched by Emer from the embrace of Fand, we know from Conchubar in *On Baile's Strand* that Cuchulain has already received the kiss of death from Aoife: "Aoife now hates you and will leave no subtlety / Unknotted that might run into a noose / About your throat. . . ."[80] And in the next play in the cycle—*The Death of Cuchulain*—we shall see the fatal consequences of that kiss.

The strands of love and death that interlink throughout Irish literature and throughout the Cuchulain plays weave their final deadly pattern in the last play in the cycle. All the women in this play have been dramatically inter-twined throughout the play cycle with Cuchulain in a sexual labyrinth that culminates in his death. Maeve, we are told, slept with Cuchulain when he was a boy: "Though when Cuchulain slept with her as a boy / She seemed pretty as a bird, she changed / She has an eye in the middle of her forehead."[81] Eithne Inguba, who delivers the call to battle in a letter while in a state of trance induced by Maeve, has been, we know, Cuchulain's mistress. And Aoife, who presides over the ceremony of death at the pillar-stone, had been sexually mastered by Cuchulain years before:

> AOIFE: I seemed invulnerable; you took my sword,
>   You threw me on the ground and left me there,
>   I searched the mountain for your sleeping-place
>   And laid my virgin body at your side,
>   And yet, because you had left me, hated you,
>   And thought that I would kill you in your sleep,
>   And yet begot a son that night between
>   Two black thorn-trees.[82]

Finally, the Morrigu, the Goddess of Death and Battle who appears in *The Death of Cuchulain*, is but another manifestation of the Hawk-Woman who seduced Cuchulain in *At the Hawk's Well*. Just as the Hawk-Woman danced the dance of seduction which aroused Cuchulain in that play, the Morrigu presides over the dance of death which we witness at the end of *The Death of Cuchulain*: "I arranged the dance." The Hawk-Woman, furthermore, is but another avatar of Fand, who, like the Hawk-Woman, excels in the seductive dance which draws men from the hearth.

In short, all of the Masks of the various fatal women that we see throughout the play cycle, dissolve ultimately into one great Mask—a Mask that represents the fatal beauty of Ireland herself. And as already stated, Yeats's use of the stone symbolism throughout the play cycle strongly suggests that he saw the beauty of the Women of the Sidhe as symbolic of the fatal beauty of Inisfail herself. Since Yeats himself links the Cuchulain plays with the Easter Rising by mentioning Pearse and his comrades at the end of the last play, it is clear that he felt both Cuchulain and the 1916 poets were motivated by that search for beauty which has shaped the imagination of Irish poet patriots over the years. Moreover, it seems clear that Yeats, like the Irish poets of old and the 1916 poets, felt that the "terrible beauty" of that search could best be symbolized by the Mask of a beautiful but fatal woman. By using this ancient poetic device, Yeats reaffirmed his connections with the literary traditions of the great Irish tapestry and that "unbroken legacy of Irish thought." The imaginative power of the feminine Mask tradition and its connection with Irish nationality is emphasized in Pearse's essay "The Spiritual Nation," written just three months before his execution:

> When I was a child I believed that there was actually a woman called Erin, and had Mr. Yeats' "Kathleen Ni Houlihan" been then written and had I seen it, I should have taken it not as an allegory, but as a representation of a thing that migh happen any day in any house. This I no longer believe as a physical possibility, . . . But I believe that there is really a spiritual

tradition which is the soul of Ireland, the thing which makes Ireland a living nation, and that there is such a spiritual tradition corresponding to true nationality. . . . The spiritual thing which is the essential thing in nationality would seem to reside chiefly in language (if by language we understand literature and folk-lore as well as sounds and idioms), and to be preserved chiefly by language; but it reveals itself in all the arts, all the institutions, all the inner life, all the actions and goings forth of the nation.[83]

At the end of *The Death of Cuchulain*, just after Cuchulain has been killed, Yeats produces from his gallery of feminine Masks a Mask that is diametrically opposed to all of the Masks we have seen throughout the play cycle—the Mask of the harlot:

> The harlot sang to the beggar-man
> I meet them face to face
> Conall, Cuchulain, Usna's boys,
> All that most ancient race;
> Maeve had three in an hour, they say.
> I adore those clever eyes,
> Those muscular bodies, but can get
> No grip upon their thighs. . . .
> What stood in the Post Office
> With Pearse and Connolly?
> What comes out of the mountain
> Where men first shed their blood?
> Who thought Cuchulain till it seemed
> He stood where they stood?[84]

Yet this Mask too seems to symbolize Ireland. If this is so, then Yeats, here as elsewhere, is sticking close to Irish literary tradition, for, within that tradition, a country that is ruled by a usurper or one that changes rulers frequently is called a harlot *(meirdreac)*.[85] Keating, in the seventeenth century, uses this term to describe the ravishing of Ireland by England in his poem, "A Banba Bog-om Dona Duaibseac [To Lonely Mournful Ireland]": "'S ataoi, a meirdreac [and you are but a harlot],"[86] and Pearse, three hundred years later, uses the same term to capture modern Ireland's defilement at the hands of the British. By 1939, when Yeats wrote *The Death of Cuchulain*, England no longer ruled Ireland (except for the six counties in the North), and I believe Yeats used the image of the harlot in this play to suggest the tendency of some of the modern Irish to betray the spiritual ideals for which the Rebellion was fought. Furthermore, Yeats's stage directions, which place the harlot in a modern Irish market place—"some Irish fair of our own day"[87]—clearly suggest that he had Pearse's exact words in mind. As mentioned in Chapter 2, Pearse wrote in "From a Hermitage": "Is not Ireland's body given up to the pleasure of another, and is not Ireland's honour for sale in the market places?" Critics, however, in their discussion of the harlot image in the play, are unaware that Yeats is using a term that has been used by other Irish poets and patriots before him. F. A. Wilson discusses the image of the harlot in the terms of neo-Platonic and Oriental philosophy,[88] while Helen Vendler believes that Yeats uses the harlot to explore the value of the images projected by the imagination.[89] While both these discussions are interesting, they overlook the Irish tapestry to which Yeats turned again and again for his images and symbols. Reg Skene does suggest that the harlot may represent modern Ireland[89] but, like Vendler and Wilson, is unaware that in using such a term for Ireland Yeats was acting within the Irish literary tradition.

The grotesque image of the harlot, however, is dwarfed by the hypnotic images of the Sidhe that fill the Cuchulain plays, and it is these latter images that are the most memorable. I believe that Yeats knew that, despite the tendency of some of the modern Irish "to fumble in a greasy till," there would always be Irish poets and patriots who would be drawn to the noble images of Ireland embodied in the Masks of the Sidhe and would fight to preserve those images.

The relationship between Cuchulain and the Woman of the Sidhe in the Cuchulain play cycle, then, symbolically suggests the relationship between the 1916 poets and the Black Rose. Both Cuchulain and the 1916 poets were drawn to the irresistible beauty of their Muse and that Muse as "daimon" leads the individual to his heroic Mask. For men like Cuchulain and the 1916 poets, beauty was all. Cuchulain, mortally wounded and about to have his throat cut, is still drawn to the beauty of Aoife's veil, which she winds around him: "But do not spoil your veil / Your veils are beautiful, some with threads of gold."[91] As Bloom points out, at the end of *The Death of Cuchulain* the "self's imaginings still matter, and beauty has not died of beauty, but can still be thought and seen. Cuchulain with six mortal wounds remains a Last Romantic."[92] Like Cuchulain, the 1916 poets remained to the end "Last Romantics," writing letters and poems in their jail cells awaiting execution. Pearse's last poem, written in his death cell at Kilmainham jail, reflects this Romantic spirit:

> The beauty of the world hath made me sad,
> This beauty that will pass;
> Sometimes my heart hath shaken with great joy
> To see a squirrel leaping in a tree,
> Or a red lady-bird upon a stalk,
> Or little rabbits in a field at evening,
> Lit by a slanting sun,
> Or some green hill where shadows drifted by
> Some quiet hill where mountainy man hath sown
> And soon would reap; near to the gate of Heaven;
> Or children with bare feet upon the sands

Of some ebbed sea, or playing on the streets
of little towns in Connacht,
Things young and happy,
And then my heart hath told me:
These things will pass,
Will pass and change, will die and be no more,
Things bright and green, things young and happy;
And I have gone upon my way
Sorrowful.[93]

In *The Only Jealousy of Emer* Fand had promised Cuchulain that, if he would make her complete by granting her a kiss, "nothing but beauty" would remain. For the 1916 poets who granted that kiss to the Black Rose, Fand's prophecy came true, for now, seventy years after the Easter Rising, it is only the poetry of the Rising that remains. In the *Tain* it is the fertile plains of Breslec Mor and the "fiery flickering of gold weapons in the eveing sunset clouds"[94] that remain in our memory long after images of dead warriors have faded. So too it is the spiritual faith and the fiery words of Pearse and his comrades we remember and not the firing squads which ended their lives. Only the beauty of Easter remains, its lyrical passion preserved forever in the Masks and Images of Yeats's poetry and plays—the greatest Irish tapestry of all.

Notes

Introduction

1. W. B. Yeats, "A General Introduction for my Work," in W. B. Yeats, *Essays and Introductions* (New York: Macmillan, 1961), p. 513.

2. For a detailed discussion of these associations, see Chapter 2 of this study. For a representative view of critical discussion on the stone symbol, see William Irwin Thompson, *The Imagination of an Insurrection* (New York: Oxford University Press, 1967), p. 156; A. Norman Jeffares, *W. B. Yeats: Man and Poet* (New Haven: Yale University Press, 1949), p. 187; Morton Irving Seiden, *William Butler Yeats: The Poet as a Mythmaker* (New York: Cooper Square, 1975), p. 159.

3. A great deal of critical discussion has been devoted to the evolution of Yeats's "Doctrine of the Mask" and to a consideration of the individuals who most influenced Yeats's theories. While critics generally agree that during the course of its evolution, Yeats's "Doctrine of the Mask" was influenced by Blake, Dowden, Wilde, Madame Blavatsky and others, there has been no agreement regarding the "origins" of Yeats's theory. Norman Jeffares discusses at length the biographical evolution of Yeats's Mask but fails to connect it with Irish fairylore. See Norman Jeffares, *The Circus Animals* (California: Stanford University Press, 1970), pp. 3–14.

4. Yeats, *Autobiographies* (London: Macmillan, 1955), p. 379.

5. Yeats, "The Statues," in *The Poems of W. B. Yeats*, ed. Richard J. Finneran (New York: Macmillan, 1983), 25–26. All further citations will be from this edition of the text except where otherwise noted.

6. In a letter to Edith Shackleton Heald, Yeats, referring to his poem "The Statues," writes: "Cuchulain is in the last stanza because Pearse and some of his followers had a cult of him. The Government has put a statue of Cuchulain in the rebuilt post office to commemorate this." See W. B. Yeats, *The Letters*, ed. Allan Wade (New York: Macmillan, 1955), p. 911.

7. See Peter Ure, *Towards a Mythology* (New York: Russell & Russell, 1967), pp. 15–27; T. R. Henn, *The Lonely Tower* (London: Methuen, 1965), pp. 1–22; Richard Ellman, *Yeats: The Man and the Masks* (New York: Norton, 1979), pp. 169–79.

8. *Tain Bo Cuailnge*, trans. Thomas Kinsella (London: Oxford University Press, 1972), p. 27.

9. Lady Gregory, trans., *Cuchulain of Muirthemne* (Buckinghamshire: Colin Smythe, 1970), p. 38.

10. Aodh de Blacam, *Gaelic Literature Surveyed* (Dublin: Talbot Press, 1929), p. 313.

11. Ann Ross, *Everyday Life of the Pagan Celts* (London: Batsford, 1970), p. 188. For a detailed discussion of the Mask motif in Celtic art, see Chapter 2 of this study.

12. Ibid., p. 193.

13. Yeats, *Essays*, pp. 226–27.

14. F. X. Martin, "Myth, Fact, and Mystery," *Studia Hibernica* 7 (1967): 10.

15. Yeats, *Poems*, 10–11.

16. P. Browne, ed., *The Collected Works of Padraic H. Pearse* (Dublin: Phoenix, 1917), p. xviii.

17. Ibid., p. xix.

Chapter 1. The Gaelic Tradition

1. Padraic H. Pearse, *The Complete Works of P. H. Pearse* (Dublin: Phoenix, 1917), p. 323. In the poem, Ireland, personified as a woman (an ancient poetic tradition continued by Yeats and the 1916 poets) is speaking. By comparing herself to the Old Woman of Beare, the persona of an Old Irish anonymous lyric written in the tenth century, the speaker emphasizes the timeless quality of her national existence. The Old Irish poem, with an accompanying English translation, appears in *A Golden Treasury of Irish Poetry*, eds. David Greene and Frank O'Connor (London: Macmillan, 1967), p. 48.

2. Yeats, p. 182.

3. Yeats, *Letters*, p. 911.

4. Yeats, *The Collected Plays of W. B. Yeats* (New York: Macmillan, 1953), p. 446.

5. Yeats, *Autobiographies*, p. 152.

6. *Tain Bo Cuailnge*, trans. Thomas Kinsella (London: Oxford University Press, 1972), p. ix.

7. Yeats, *Plays*, p. 185.

8. Critics agree that Yeats also used Cuchulain to mirror aspects of his own personal struggles.

9. Lady Gregory, trans., *Cuchulain of Muirthemne* p. 38. Cuchulain refers many times to his talents as a poet. He reminds Emer that he was raised "among poets and learned men . . . so that I have all their manners and their gifts" (p. 37).

10. Ibid., p. 38.

11. Ibid., p. 38.

12. Yeats, *The Variorum Edition of the Poems*, ed. Peter Allt and Russell K. Alspach (New York: Macmillan, 1957), p. 539.

13. Yeats, "Note" to Lady Gregory's *Cuchulain of Muirthemne*, p. 264.

14. Ibid., p. 265.

15. *Fled Bricrend*, trans. George Henderson (London: Irish Texts Society, 1899), p. xxv.

16. The *Book of Kells* belongs to a distinctive group of "Insular" illuminated manuscripts whose connections are chiefly in Ireland, Scotland and in the monastery of Lindisfarne in the north of England. The Book is a Latin copy of the four Gospels written in Irish script and is filled with strange hieratic figures, fantastic elongated beasts and intricate animated initials. It is one of the most exquisite manuscripts of the Middle Ages.

17. Sean Cronin, *Our Own Red Blood* (Dublin: Wolfe Tone Society, 1966), p. 13.

18. Yeats, *Letters*, p. 613.

19. Yeats, *Essays and Introductions* (New York: Macmillan, 1961) p. 515.

20. Raymond J. Porter, *P. H. Pearse* (New York: Twayne), p. 101.

21. Yeats, *Essays*, p. 518.

22. Yeats, *Essays*, p. 431.

23. Yeats, *The Speckled Bird*, ed. W. H. O'Donnell (Canada: Macmillan and Stewart, 1976), pp. 98–99.

24. John Rhys, *Lectures on the Origin and Growth of Celtic Heathendom* (London: Williams & Norgate, 1892), p. 27.

25. Lady Gregory, *Cuchulain of Muirthemne*, p. 35.

26. R. A. S. Macalister, *The Archeology of Ireland* (New York: Benjamin Blom, 1972), p. 348.

27. See *Tain*, p. 150.

28. de Blacam, *Gaelic Literature Surveyed*, p. 21.

29. Yeats, *Essays*, p. 514.

30. Yeats, *Essays*, p. 514.

31. James Carney, "Old Ireland and Her Poetry," in *Old Ireland*, ed. Robert McNally, S. J. (New York: Fordham University Press, 1965), p. 165.

32. William Irwin Thompson, *The Imagination of an Insurrection: Dublin, Easter, 1916* (New York: Oxford University Press, 1967), p. 119.

33. Kinsella, *Tain*, p. xvi.

34. The fascination with Mask and Image that pervades the poems, plays, and essays of the poet rebels has not been explored by scholars to date.

35. Yeats, *Autobiographies*, pp. 193–94.

36. Pearse et al., *The 1916 Poets*, ed. Desmond Ryan (Connecticut: Greenwood Press, 1963), p. 125.

37. Thompson, *Imagination of an Insurrection*, p. 235.

38. Richard J. Loftus, "Yeats and the Easter Rising: A Study in Ritual," *Arizona Quarterly* 16 (1960): 171. Loftus cites the following note which Yeats appended to "Three Songs to the Same Tune," as proof that Yeats's nationalism and his dramatic art were closely related: "A nation should be like an audience in some great theatre— 'in the theater' said Victor Hugo, 'the mob becomes a people'—watching the drama of its own history . . . ; that sacred drama must to all native eyes and ears become the greatest of parables."

39. Yeats, *Essays*, pp. 513–14.

40. Ibid., p. 173.

41. Seamus Heaney, *Preoccupations* (New York: Farrar, Straus & Giroux, 1980), p. 41.

42. Ibid., p. 41.

43. Yeats, *Plays*, p. 446.

44. W. B. Yeats, Preface to *Cuchulain* by Lady Gregory, p. 14.

45. Ibid., p. 12.

46. Ibid., p. 13.

47. Yeats, *Essays*, p. 180.

48. Ibid., p. 180.

49. Denis de Rougement, *Love in the Western World* (New York: Harper & Row, 1974).

50. George Sigerson, *Bards of the Gael and Gall* (London: Fisher Unwin, 1907), p. 112.

51. Yeats, *Essays*, p. 180.

52. Yeats, *Variorum*, pp. 811–12.

53. Porter, *P. H. Pearse*, p. 56.

54. Lady Gregory, *Cuchulain*, p. 15.

55. Pearse et al., *1916 Poets*, p. 201.

56. Sean Cronin, *Our Own Red Blood* (Dublin: Wolfe Tone Society, 1966), p. 14.

57. Yeats, *Plays*, p. 54.

58. Ibid., p. 53.

59. Yeats, *Essays*, p. 519.

60. Porter, *Pearse*, p. 56.

61. Herbert Howarth, *The Irish Writers 1880–1940* (London: Rockliff, 1958), p. 127.

62. Yeats, *Mythologies* (New York: Macmillan, 1959), p. 163.

63. Pearse et al., *1916 Poets*, p. 204.

64. Ibid., p. 202.

65. Ibid., p. 212.

66. Ibid., p. 19.

67. Ibid., p. 20.

68. Ibid., p. 53.

69. Ibid., p. 141.

70. Yeats, *Essays*, p. 517.

71. Bobby Sands, *Prison Poems* (Dublin: Sinn Fein, 1981), p. 78.

72. Ibid., p. 78.

73. Ibid., p. 31.

74. Ibid., p. 78.

75. Heaney, Poems 1965–1975 (New York: Farrar, Straus, and Giroux, 1980), p. 200.

76. Ibid., p. 196.

77. Ibid., p. 200.

78. Ibid., p. 195.

79. "The Old Woman of Beare," from *The Penguin Book of Irish Verse*, ed. Brendan Kennelly (Middlesex: Penguin Books, 1970), p. 62.

80. Andre Malraux, *Antimemoires*, as quoted in Gerhard Herm, *The Celts* (London: Weidenfeld and Nicholson, 1976), p. 141.

81. Heaney, *Poems*, p. 171.

82. Carney, *Old Ireland*, p. 151.

83. Ibid., p. 152.

84. Lady Gregory, *Cuchulain*, p. 182.

85. Pearse et al., *1916 Poets*, p. 196.

86. Carney, *Old Ireland*, p. 152.

87. Ibid., p. 153.

88. Lady Gregory, *Cuchulain*, p. 15.

89. Macalister, *Archaeology*, p. 253.

90. P. W. Joyce, *A Social History of Ancient Ireland* (Dublin: Longmans, Green, 1906), p. 534.

91. Pearse et al., *1916 Poets*, p. 196.

92. Cronin, *Our Own Red Blood* p. 26.

93. Kennelly, *Irish Verse*, p. 29.

94. Ibid., p. 29.

95. Ibid., p. 29.

96. Ibid., p. 29.

97. Yeats, Preface to *Cuchulain* by Lady Gregory, p. 14.

98. Yeats, *Essays*, p. 182.

99. Ibid., p. 182.

100. Kennelly, *Irish Verse*, p. 78.

101. Porter, *Pearse*, p. 150.

102. Ibid., p. 100.

103. Pearse, *Complete Works*, p. 54.

104. Ibid., p. 60.

105. Ibid., p. 54.

106. Ibid., p. 54.

107. Joseph Sheridan Le Fanu, *The Poems of Joseph Sheridan Le Fanu* (Dublin: James Duffy, 1904), p. 108.

108. Ibid., p. 108.

109. Richard Ellmann, *The Identity of Yeats* (New York: Oxford University Press, 1970), p. 214.

110. Yeats, *Letters*, p. 917.

111. Ellman, *Identity of Yeats*, p. 213.

112. Wade, *Letters*, p. 922.

113. Yeats, *Essays*, p. 173.

114. Ibid., p. 173.

115. Yeats, Preface to *Cuchulain* by Lady Gregory, p. 15.

116. Yeats, *Essays*, p. 173.

117. Lady Gregory, *Cuchulain*, p. 16.

118. Yeats, *Essays*, p. 235.

119. Ibid., p. 235.

Chapter 2. The Search for Beauty

1. Yeats, *Essays and Introductions*, p. 516.

2. Ann Ross, *Everyday Life of the Pagan Celts* (London: Batsford, 1970), p. 188, 193.

3. R. A. S. Macalister, *The Archeology of Ireland* (New York: Benjamin Blom, 1972), p. 357.

4. Nora Chadwick, *The Celts* (London: Pelican, 1970), pp. 159–60.

5. Yeats, *Autobiographies*, p. 269.

6. Ross, p. 157.

7. Gale C. Schricker, *A New Species of Man* (Lewisburg: Bucknell University Press, 1982), pp. 17–18.

8. Gerhard Herm, *The Celts* (London: Weidenfeld and Nicolson, 1975), p. 152 (illustration No. 9).

9. Lady Gregory, *Cuchulain*, p. 169.

10. *Tain*, p. 150.

11. Ross, p. 182.

12. Macalister, p. 355.

13. Sigerson, *Bards of the Gael and Gall*, p. 2.

14. Ibid., p. 2.

15. de Blacam, p. 8.

16. Ibid., p. 8.

17. de Blacam, p. 8.

18. Ibid., p. 8.

19. Ibid., p. 9.

20. Ibid., p. 9.

21. Yeats, "No Second Troy," 8.

22. Yeats, *Essays*, p. 226.

23. Yeats, *Autobiographies*, p. 379.

24. Yeats, *Plays* p. 186.

25. Yeats, "Irish Fairies, Ghosts, Witches," *Lucifer* (15 January 1889): 404.

26. Yeats, *Autobiographies*, p. 493.

27. Thompson, *Imagination of an Insurrection*, p. 143.

28. Porter, *P. H. Pearse*, p. 57.

29. Liam Miller, *The Dolmen Press Yeats Centenary Papers* (Dublin: Dolmen Press, 1968), p. 101.

30. Yeats, *Essays*, p. 515.

31. Geoffrey Keating, *The General History of Ireland* as quoted in de Blacam, *Gaelic Literature Surveyed* p. 6. Keating, known as the Irish Herodotus, links ancient and modern Ireland. His important book *The General History of Ireland* is one of the most important sources of information about medieval Ireland and at the same time marks the beginning of modern Irish literature. The book was written before 1640, during the years that Keating was hiding out in the mountains and glens from the British. Both Yeats and Pearse were, of course, totally familiar with Keating's writings.

32. Pearse, as quoted by Reg Skene in *The Cuchulain Plays of W. B. Yeats* (New York: Columbia University Press, 1974), p. 19.

33. Pearse, *Collected Works*, pp. 224–29. Pearse repeats a phrase which Keating uses to describe Ireland. Keating spoke of Ireland as "domhan beag inniti fein" (a little world in herself). Pearse notes that historically it has been characteristic of Irish-speaking men that when they thought of Ireland they thought less of its "outer forms and pomps than of the inner thing which was its soul." Pearse adds that "Irish nationality is an ancient spiritual tradition, one of the oldest and most august traditions in the world." Thus it is a precious jewel. Pearse frequently quoted Keating, whom he described in "From a Hermitage" as "the greatest of Irish Nationalist poets."

34. de Blacam, *Gaelic Literature Surveyed*, p. 7.

35. Ibid., p. 7.

36. de Blacam, *Gaelic Literature*, p. 28. In ancient Ireland the Druid and the poet were one, and literature had religious and magical significance. Legend has it that St. Patrick

required the poets, with the acceptance of Christianity, to forego many of their ancient magical practices, such as "imbas forosna," a magical method of inducing second sight.

37. Ibid., p. 28.

38. de Blacam, p. 17.

39. Eleanor Knott, *Irish Syllabic Poetry* (Dublin: Dublin Institute of Advanced Studies, 1957), p. 72.

40. de Blacam, p. 125.

41. Ibid., p. 127.

42. Kennelly, *Irish Verse*, p. 33.

43. de Blacam, p. 281.

44. Ibid., p. 281.

45. Yeats, *Essays*, p. 519.

46. Ibid., p. 282.

47. Ibid., p. 282.

48. Ibid., p. 283.

49. Ibid., p. 283.

50. de Blacam, p. 285.

51. Yeats, *Autobiographies*, p. 464.

52. The Battle of Kinsale was fought in the winter of 1601. It was a disaster for the Irish and marked the end of the Gaelic aristocratic order. Red Hugh O'Donnell went to Spain to seek help after the battle but was poisoned by agents of the British. Later, other members of the Gaelic aristocracy went into exile on the continent. Their departure from Ireland is known as "the flight of the Wild Geese," and Yeats refers to this event in his poem, "September 1913."

53. Pearse, *Collected Works*, p. 153. As we shall see in Chapter 3, Yeats, who was thoroughly familiar with Keating's works, uses the term "harlot" in much the same way as Keating and Pearse.

54. Ibid. p. 154.

55. Pearse, *Collected Works*, p. 150.

56. Ibid., p. 149.

57. Johann Norstedt, *Thomas MacDonagh* (Charlottesville: University Press of Virginia, 1980), p. 2.

58. Pearse et al., *The 1916 Poets*, ed. Desmond Ryan (Connecticut: Greenwood Press, 1963), p. 76.

59. Ibid., p. 180.

60. Osborn Bergin, *Irish Bardic Poetry* (Dublin: Dublin Institute for Advanced Studies, 1970), p. 4.

61. Lady Gregory, *Cuchulain*, p. 199.

62. James Joyce, *Ulysses* (New York: Random House, 1961), p. 4.

63. Kenneth Hurlstone Jackson, *The Oldest Irish Tradition: A Window on the Iron Age* (Cambridge: Cambridge University Press, 1964), p. 27.

64. Yeats, *Autobiographies*, p. 263.

65. Yeats, *Essays*, p. 159.

66. Yeats, *Autobiographies*, p. 270.

67. Yeats, *Autobiographies*, p. 272.

68. Ibid., p. 273.

69. Ruth Dudley Edwards, *Patrick Pearse: The Triumph of Failure* (London: Faber, 1979), p. 338.

70. Ibid., p. 278.

71. Yeats, *Variorum* p. 788.

72. Thompson, *Imagination of an Insurrection*, pp. 114–15.

73. Ibid., p. 129.

74. Ibid., p. 131.

75. Edwards, *Pearse*, p. 227.
76. Thompson, *Imagination of an Insurrection*, p. 77.
77. Pearse et al., *The 1916 Poets*, p. 13.
78. Porter, *Pearse*, p. 62.
79. Ibid., p. 62.
80. Edwards, *Pearse*, p. 284.
81. Ibid., p. 252.
82. de Blacam, p. 120.
83. Porter, *Pearse*, p. 61.
84. de Blacam, p. 120.
85. Ibid., p. 120.
86. Porter, *Pearse*, p. 62.
87. de Blacam, p. 120.
88. Yeats, *Essays*, p. 428.
89. Ibid., p. 213.
90. Ibid., p. 213.
91. Ibid., p. 248.
92. J. Markale, *Celtic Civilization* (London: Gordon & Cremonesi, 1978), p. 223.
93. Ibid., p. 225.
94. Yeats, *Plays*, p. 446.
95. Yeats, *Autobiographies*, p. 465.
96. Yeats, *Essays*, p. 321.
97. Yeats, *Autobiographies*, p. 457.
98. Pearse et al., *The 1916 Poets*, p. 16.
99. Ibid., p. 82.
100. Ibid., p. 90.
101. Ibid., p. 188.
102. Yeats, *Plays*, p. 444.
103. Yeats, *Poems*, p. 159.
104. Pearse et al., *The 1916 Poets*, p. 164.
105. Yeats, *Plays*, p. 93.
106. Yeats, *Autobiographies*, p. 471.
107. Yukio Mishima, *Sun and Steel* (New York: Grove, 1970), p. 21. Mishima writes: "A hostility towards the sun was my only rebellion against the spirit of the age. I hankered after Novalis's night and Yeatsian Irish twilights."
108. Ibid., p. 54.
109. Ibid., p. 49.
110. Ibid., p. 55.
111. Yeats, *Essays and Introductions*, p. 212.
112. Pearse, *Collected Works*, p. 99.
113. Lady Gregory, *Cuchulain*, p. 59.
114. Ibid., p. 59.
115. *Tain*, p. 153.
116. Yeats, *Essays and Introductions*, p. 235.
117. Pearse et al., *The 1916 Poets*, p. 113.
118. Edwards, p. 162.
119. Ibid., p. 130.
120. Ibid., p. 130.
121. Yeats, *Essays*, p. 232.
122. Ibid., p. 232.
123. Lady Gregory, p. 263.
124. Mishima, p. 50.
125. Ibid., p. 50.

126. Yeats, *A Vision* (New York: Macmillan Press), p. 292.

127. Ibid., p. 293.

128. Yeats, *Essays*, p. 233.

129. Yeats, *Autobiographies*, p. 472.

130. Mary Helen Thuente, *W. B. Yeats* (New Jersey: Gill & Macmillan, 1980), p. 259.

131. Thompson, p. 22.

132. Ibid., p. 22.

133. Thuente, p. 253.

134. Ibid., p. 251.

135. Ibid., p. 252.

136. Yeats, *Variorum*, p. 793.

137. Thuente, p. 252.

138. Yeats, *Essays*, p. 255.

139. Robert O'Driscoll, *An Ascendancy of the Heart: Ferguson and the Beginnings of Modern Irish Literature in English* (Toronto: Phoenix, 1976), p. 53.

140. Michael Yeats, "W. B. Yeats and Irish Folk Song," *Southern Folk-Lore Quarterly* 31 (June 1966): 153–78.

141. Sean Lucy, "Metre and Movement in Anglo-Irish Verse," *Irish University Review* 8/2 (Autumn 1978): 151–77.

142. Yeats, *Essays*, p. 523.

143. Yeats, as quoted in Lady Gregory *Seventy Years* (New York: Macmillan, 1976), p. 549.

144. Yeats, *Essays*, p. 523.

145. Charles Donahue, "Beowulf and Christian Tradition: A Reconsideration from a Celtic Stance," *Traditio* 21 (1965): 59.

146. F. X. Martin, "Myth, Fact, and Mystery," 10.

147. Yeats, *Autobiographies*, p. 135.

148. Ibid., pp. 286–87.

149. Ibid., p. 138.

150. Seiden, *The Poet as a Mythmaker*, p. 209.

151. Yeats, *Mythologies*, p. 334.

152. Yeats, *A Vision*, p. 81.

153. For a representative view of critical discussion on the stone symbol, see Jeffares, *W. B. Yeats: Man and Poet*, p. 187; Seiden, *William Butler Yeats: The Poet as a Mythmaker*, p. 159; Thompson, *The Imagination of an Insurrection*, p. 156; John Unterecker, *A Reader's Guide to William Butler Yeats* (New York: Octagon, 1971), p. 161.

154. Geoffrey Keating, *The General History of Ireland*, trans. Dermitius O'Connor (London: Bettenham, 1723), p. 73.

155. Ibid., p. 73.

156. Yeats, *Autobiographies*, p. 488.

157. Yeats, *Essays*, p. 258.

158. Yeats, *Variorum*, p. 188.

159. Yeats, *Mythologies* pp. 220–21

160. Ibid., pp. 259–260.

161. Jeffares, *W. B. Yeats: Man and Poet*, p. 140.

162. Yeats, *Essays*, p. 161.

163. Yeats, *Autobiographies*, p. 490.

164. Pearse et al., *The 1916 Poets*, p. 28.

165. Yeats, *A Vision*, p. 66.

166. Seiden, p. 199.

167. Ibid., p. 199.

168. Yeats, *Autobiographies*, p. 254.

169. Seiden, p. 44.

170. Ibid., p. 44.

171. Ibid., p. 47.
172. Ibid., p. 51.
173. Ibid., p. 51.
174. Norstedt, *Thomas MacDonagh*, p. 143.
175. Pearse et al., *The 1916 Poets*, p. 122.
176. Norstedt, p. 55.
177. Ibid., p. 3.
178. Yeats, *Mythologies*, p. 335.
179. Cronin, *Our Own Red Blood*, p. 8.
180. Norstedt, p. 129.
181. Plato, *The Works of Plato*, trans. B. A. Jowett (New York: Dial Press, 1967), p. 216.
182. Yeats, *Variorum*, p. 577.
183. Norstedt, p. 121.
184. Keating, p. 73.
185. Yeats, *Essays*, p. 249.
186. Ibid., p. 521.
187. Edwards, p. 133.
188. Pearse et al., *The 1916 Poets*, p. 132.
189. Yeats, *Essays*, p. 230.
190. Pearse et al., *The 1916 Poets*, p. 86.
191. Ibid., p. 187.
192. Ibid., p. 170.
193. Lieberson, p. 10.
194. Peter McBrien, "Poets of the Insurrection," *Studies* (December 1916): 538.
195. Edwards, p. 278.
196. Pearse et al., *The 1916 Poets*, p. 181.
197. Yeats, *A Vision*, p. 82.
198. Edwards, p. 128.
199. Ibid., p. 127.
200. Ibid., p. 175.
201. F. X. Martin, *Leaders and Men of the Easter Rising* (London: Methuen, 1967), p. 160.
202. Porter, p. 15.
203. Porter, *Pearse*, p. 15.
204. Ibid., p. 15.
205. Yeats, *Autobiographies*, p. 272.
206. Edwards, *Pearse*, p. 192.
207. Pearse et al., *The 1916 Poets*, p. 18.
208. Yeats, *Autobiographies*, p. 189.
209. Ibid., p. 189.
210. Ibid., p. 189.
211. Yeats, *Autobiographies*, p. 273.
212. Desmond Ryan, *The Rising* (Dublin: Golden Eagle, 1949), p. 263.
213. Elizabeth, Countess of Fingall, *Seventy Years Young* (London: Collins, 1937), p. 375.
214. Porter, p. 35.
215. Oscar Wilde, "The Decay of Lying," in *The Artist as Critic: Critical Writings of Oscar Wilde*, ed. Richard Ellmann (New York: Random House, 1968), p. 307.
216. Ibid., p. 270.
217. Edwards, p. 175.
218. Pearse, *The Collected Works* (Dublin: Phoenix, 1916), p. 161.
219. Edwards, p. 177.
220. Yeats, *Plays*, p. 158.
221. Ibid., p. 159.
222. Pearse et al., *The 1916 Poets*, p. 25.

223. Edwards, p. 124.
224. Ibid., p. 278.
225. Yeats, *Plays*, p. 446.
226. Yeats, *A Vision*, p. 82.
227. Yeats, *Essays*, p. 259.
228. Ibid., p. 260.
229. Ibid., p. 254.
230. Ibid., p. 226.

Chapter 3. The Kiss of Death

1. Pearse et al., *The 1916 Poets*, p. 201.
2. The Sidhe are an appropriate symbol for Ireland because like Ireland they demand total sacrifice from those who serve them. Yeats has written many poems about the Sidhe and, in the extensive notes which appear after his poem "The Hosting of the Sidhe," he writes, "If any one becomes too much interested in them, and sees them over much, he loses all interest in ordinary things. . . ." Yeats writes of the Sidhe who inhabit the waters: "To this day the Tribes of the Goddess Danu that are in the waters beckon to men, and drown them in the waters. . . . The people of the waters have been in all ages beautiful and changeable and lascivious, or beautiful and wise and lonely."
3. Heaney, *Poems 1965–1975*, p. 200.
4. John Rees Moore, "Evolution of Myth in the Plays of W. B. Yeats," Ph.D. diss., Columbia University, 1957), p. 121.
5. Yeats, *Mythologies*, p. 233.
6. Yeats, "Irish Fairies, Ghosts, Witches," *Lucifer* (15 January 1889): 403.
7. Pearse et al., *The 1916 Poets*, p. 119.
8. Ibid., p. 125.
9. Yeats, *Poems*, p. 330.
10. Pearse et al., *The 1916 Poets*, p. 184.
11. Ibid., p. 184.
12. Ibid., p. 173.
13. Yeats, *Poems*, p. 133.
14. Pearse et al., *The 1916 Poets*, p. 55.
15. Ibid., p. 57.
16. Pearse, *Collected Works*, pp. 30–31.
17. Ibid., p. 40.
18. Ibid., p. 44.
19. Ibid., p. 19.
20. Ibid., p. 87.
21. Leonard E. Nathan, *The Tragic Drama of William Butler Yeats* (New York: Columbia University Press, 1966), p. 162.
22. Ibid., p. 163.
23. Pearse, *Collected Works*, p. 93.
24. Yeats, *Plays*, p. 162.
25. Ibid., p. 141.
26. Ibid., p. 139.
27. Ibid., p. 140.
28. Ibid., p. 137.
29. Yeats, *Poems*, p. 103.
30. Yeats, *Plays*, p. 169.
31. Ibid., p. 144.

32. There is a long episode in the *Tain* that treats Fergus's sudden impotence with Maeve in terms of sword imagery. Ailill taunts Fergus by saying to him: "Why so wild without your weapon / on heights of a certain royal belly in a certain ford / was your will worked / or your heroism an empty shout. . . ." See *Tain*, p. 104. As discussed in Chapter One, the sword has phallic implications in the love-death poetry of the 1916 rebels.

33. Yeats, *Plays*, p. 185.

34. Ibid., p. 165.

35. Ibid., p. 442.

36. Ibid., p. 442.

37. Yeats, *Essays and Introductions*, p. 234.

38. Ibid., p. 234.

39. Ibid., p. 234.

40. Yeats, *Plays*, p. 144.

41. Yeats, *Autobiographies*, p. 272.

42. Helen Hennessy Vendler, *Yeats's Vision and the Later Plays* (Cambridge, Mass.: Harvard University Press, 1963), p. 213.

43. Yeats, *Mythologies*, p. 336.

44. Ibid., p. 336.

45. Ibid., p. 336.

46. Nathan, p. 178.

47. Yeats, *Plays*, p. 158.

48. Ibid., p. 158.

49. Ibid., p. 163.

50. Ibid., p. 167.

51. Pearse, *Collected Works*, p. 241.

52. Ibid., p. 205.

53. Yeats, *Mythologies*, p. 237.

54. Yeats, *Plays*, p. 171.

55. Ibid., p. 171.

56. Pearse et al., *The 1916 Poets*, p. 13.

57. Pearse, *Collected Works*, p. 204.

58. Yeats, *Plays*, p. 172.

59. Harold Bloom, *Yeats* (New York: Oxford University Press, 1970), p. 299.

60. Yeats, *A Vision* (New York: Macmillan, 1956), p. 128.

61. Yeats, *Plays*, p. 181.

62. Yeats, *Autobiographies*, p. 274.

63. Pearse et al., *The 1916 Poets*, p. 143.

64. Ure, *Towards a Mythology*, p. 21.

65. Vendler, pp. 221–27.

66. Bloom, *Yeats*, p. 303. See also Skene, *The Cuchulain Plays of W. B. Yeats*, pp. 201–21; F. A. C. Wilson, *W. B. Yeats and Tradition* (New York: Macmillan, 1958), p. 162.

67. Bloom, p. 300.

68. Yeats, *Plays*, p. 191.

69. Ibid., pp. 191–92.

70. Ibid., p. 187.

71. Ibid., p. 190.

72. Ibid., p. 190.

73. Pearse et al., *The 1916 Poets*, p. 132.

74. Norstedt, *Thomas MacDonagh*, p. 139.

75. Pearse et al., *The 1916 Poets*, p. 26.

76. Yeats, *Plays*, p. 189.

77. Ibid., p. 191.

78. Jeffares, *W. B. Yeats: Man and Poet*, p. 45.

79. Yeats, *Poems*, p. 67.

80. Yeats, *Plays*, p. 169.

81. Yeats, *Plays*, p. 440.

82. Ibid., p. 443.

83. Pearse, *Collected Works*, pp. 300–301.

84. Yeats, *Plays*, p. 445.

85. Rev. Patrick S. Dineen, *Irish-English Dictionary* (Dublin: The Educatioinal Company of Ireland, 1927), p. 735.

86. Geoffrey Keating, *Danta Amrain is Caointe Seatruin Ceitinn* (Dublin: Conrad na Gaedilge, 1900), p. 79.

87. Yeats, *Plays*, p. 445.

88. Wilson, *W. B. Yeats and Tradition*, pp. 176–85.

89. Vendler, *Yeats's Vision and the Later Plays*, pp. 246–48.

90. Skene, *The Cuchulain Plays of W. B. Yeats*, p. 238.

91. Yeats, *Plays*, p. 442.

92. Bloom, *Yeats*, p. 432.

93. Pearse et al., *The 1916 Poets*, p. 30.

94. *Tain*, p. 140.

Select Bibliography

Works by Yeats

Autobiographies. London: Macmillan, 1955.

The Collected Plays of W. B. Yeats. New York: Macmillan, 1953.

Essays and Introductions. New York: Macmillan, 1961.

Explorations. New York: Macmillan, 1963.

"Irish Fairies, Ghosts, Witches." *Lucifer*, 15 January 1889, pp. 399–404.

The Letters of W. B. Yeats. Edited by Allan Wade. New York: Macmillan, 1955.

Mythologies. New York: Macmillan, 1959.

The Poems of W. B. Yeats. Edited by Richard J. Finneran. New York: Macmillan, 1983.

Variorum Edition of the Plays of W. B. Yeats. Edited by Russell K. Alspach. New York: Macmillan, 1966.

Variorum Edition of the Poems of W. B. Yeats. Edited by Peter Allt and Russell K. Alspach. New York: Macmillan, 1957.

A Vision. New York: Macmillan, 1956.

Secondary Sources

Bergin, Osborn. *Irish Bardic Poetry*. Dublin: Dublin Institute for Advanced Studies, 1970.

Best, R. I., and M. A. O'Brien, eds. *Leabhor Mor Whic Fhir Bhisegh Leacain*. Dublin: Stationery Office of Saorstat Eireann, 1957.

———. *Lebar Na Nuachongbala*. Dublin: Dublin Institute for Advanced Studies, 1956.

Bjersby, Birgit. *The Cuchulain Legend*. Dublin: Hodges, Figgis, 1950.

Bloom, Harold. *Yeats*. New York: Oxford University Press, 1970.

Bruford, Alan. *Gaelic Folk-Tales and Medieval Romances*. Dublin: The Folklore of Ireland Society, 1969.

Callan, Edward. *Yeats on Yeats*. Portlaoise: Dolmen, 1981.

Carney, James. "Old Ireland and Her Poetry." In *Old Ireland,* edited by Robert McNally, S. J. New York: Fordham University Press, 1965.

Chadwick, Nora. *The Celts.* London: Pelican, 1970.

Cronin, Sean. *Our Own Red Blood.* Dublin: Wolfe Tone Society, 1966.

Cross, Tom Peete, and Clark Harris Slover. *Ancient Irish Tales.* New York: Henry Holt, 1936.

de Blacam, Aodh. *Gaelic Literature Surveyed.* Dublin: Talbot Press, 1929.

Donahue, Charles. "Beowulf and Christian Tradition: A Reconsideration from a Celtic Stance." *Traditio* 21 (1965): 55–116.

Duff, Charles. *Six Days to Shake an Empire.* London: Faber, 1966.

Edwards, Ruth Dudley. *Patrick Pearse: The Triumph of Failure.* London: Faber, 1979.

Elizabeth, Countess of Fingall. *Seventy Years Young.* London: Collins, 1937.

Ellman, Richard. *The Identity of Yeats.* New York: Oxford University Press, 1954.

———. *Yeats, the Man and the Masks.* New York: E. P. Dutton, 1978.

Engleberg, Edward. *The Vast Design: Patterns in Yeats's Aesthetic.* Springfield, Ill.: C. C. Thomas, 1964.

Fitzgerald, Redmond. *Cry Blood, Cry Erin.* New York: C. N. Potter, 1966.

Flower, Robin. *The Irish Tradition.* Oxford: Clarendon Press, 1947.

Greaves, C. D. *James Connolly.* New York: International, 1971.

Green, David, and Frank O'Connor, eds. *A Golden Treasury of Irish Poetry* A.D. *600–1200.* London: Macmillan, 1967.

Greene, David. *An Anthology of Irish Literature.* New York: New York University Press, 1971.

———. *Duanaire Mheig Uidhir: The Poembook of Cu Chonnacht Mag Uidhir, Lord of Fermanagh 1566–1589.* Dublin: Dublin Institute for Advanced Studies, 1972.

———. *Irish Literature.* New York: New York University Press, 1971.

Gregory, Lady Augusta, trans. *Cuchulain of Muirthemne.* Buckinghamshire: Colin Smythe, 1970.

Hardiman, James. *Irish Minstrelsy.* London: Joseph Robbins, 1831.

Heaney, Seamus. *Poems 1965–1975.* New York: Farrar, Straus and Giroux, 1980.

Henderson, George, trans. *Fled Bricrend.* London: Irish Texts Society, 1899.

Henn, T. R. *The Lonely Tower.* New York: Barnes and Noble, 1965.

Herm, Gerhard. *The Celts.* London: Weidenfeld and Nicolson, 1975.

Hoffman, Daniel. *Barbarous Knowledge.* New York: Oxford University Press, 1961.

Hone, Joseph. *W. B. Yeats 1865–1939*. New York: St. Martins, 1962.

Hough, Graham. *The Last Romantics*. New York: Barnes and Noble, 1961.

Howarth, Herbert, *The Irish Writers 1880–1940*. London: Rockliff, 1958.

Jackson, Kenneth Hurlstone. *The Oldest Irish Tradition: A Window on the Iron Age*. Cambridge: Cambridge University Press, 1964.

Jeffares, A. Norman. *A Commentary on the Collected Poems of W. B. Yeats*. California: Stanford University Press, 1968.

————. *W. B. Yeats, Man and Poet*. New Haven: Yale University Press, 1949.

Joyce, James. *Ulysses*. New York: Random House, 1961.

Joyce, P. W. *A Social History of Ancient Ireland*. Dublin: Longmans, Green, 1906.

Keating, Geoffrey. The General History of Ireland. Translated by Dermitius O'Connor. London: Bettenham, 1723.

Kennelly, Brendan. *The Penguin Book of Irish Verse*. Middlesex: Penguin, 1970.

Kinsella, Thomas, trans. *Tain Bo Cuailnge*. London: Oxford University Press, 1972.

Knott, Eleanor. *Irish Syllabic Poetry*. Dublin: Dublin Institute for Advanced Studies, 1957.

Le Fanu, Joseph Sheridan. *The Poems of Joseph Sheridan Le Fanu*. Dublin: James Duffy and Co., Ltd., 1904.

Lieberson, Goddard. *The Irish Uprising*. New York: Macmillan, 1966.

Loftus, Richard J. "Yeats and the Easter Rising: A Study in Ritual." *Arizona Quarterly*, 2d ser., 16 (Summer 1960): 168–77.

Loomis, Roger Sherman. *Celtic Myth & Arthurian Romance*. New York: Columbia University Press, 1927.

Lucy, Sean. "Metre and Movement in Anglo-Irish Verse." *Irish University Review*, 2d ser., 8 (Autumn 1978): 151–77.

Macalister, R. A. S. *The Archeology of Ireland*. New York: Benjamin Blom, 1972.

McBrien, Peter. "Poets of the Insurrection." *Studies* (December 1916): 537–49.

Markale, J. *Celtic Civilization*. London: Gordon and Cremonesi, 1978.

Martin, F. X. *Leaders and Men of the Easter Rising*. London: Meuthen, 1967.

Melchiori, Giorgio. *The Whole Mystery of Art*. New York: Macmillan, 1961.

Miller, Liam. *The Dolmen Press Yeats Centenary Papers*. Dublin: Dolmen, 1968.

Mishima, Yukio. *Sun and Steel*. New York: Grove, 1970.

Nathan, Leonard. *The Tragic Drama of William Butler Yeats*. New York: Columbia University Press, 1966.

Norstedt, Johann. *Thomas MacDonagh*. Charlottesville: University Press of Virginia, 1980.

O'Driscoll, Robert. *An Ascendancy of the Heart: Ferguson and the Beginnings of Modern Irish Literature in English*. Toronto: Phoenix, 1976.

Pearse, Padraic. *The Collected Works of Padraic H. Pearse*. Edited by P. Browne. Dublin: Phoenix, 1917.

———. *The Complete Works of P. H. Pearse*. Dublin: Phoenix, 1917.

Pearse, Padraic, Thomas MacDonagh, and Joseph Plunkett. *The 1916 Poets*. Edited by Desmond Ryan. Westport, Conn.: Greenwood Press, 1963.

Plato. *The Works of Plato*. Translated by B. A. Jowett. New York: Dial, 1967.

Porter, Raymond J. *P. H. Pearse*. New York: Twayne, 1973.

Rhys, John. *Lectures on the Origin and Growth of Celtic Heathendom*. London: Williams and Norgate, 1892.

Ross, Ann. *Everyday Life of the Pagan Celts*. London: Batsford, 1970.

Ryan, Desmond. *The Rising*. Dublin: Golden Eagle, 1949.

Sands, Bobby. *Prison Poems*. Dublin: Sinn Fein, 1981.

Schricker, Gale C. *A New Species of Man*. Lewisburg, Penn.: Bucknell University Press, 1982.

Seiden, Morton Irving. *The Poet as a Mythmaker*. New York: Cooper Square, 1975.

Skene, Reg. *The Cuchulain Plays of W. B. Yeats*. New York: Columbia University Press, 1914.

Thompson, W. I. *The Imagination of an Insurrection*. New York: Oxford University Press, 1967.

Thuente, Mary Helen. *W. B. Yeats*. Dublin: Gill & Macmillan, 1980.

Vendler, Helen Hennessy. *Yeats's Vision and the Later Plays*. Cambridge, Mass.: Harvard University Press, 1963.

Wilde, Oscar. "The Decay of Lying." In *The Artist as Critic: Critical Writings of Oscar Wilde*, edited by Richard Ellmann. New York: Random House, 1968.

Wilson, F. A. C,. *W. B. Yeats and Tradition*. New York: Macmillan, 1958.

Yeats, Michael. "W. B. Yeats and Irish Folk Song." *Southern Folklore Quarterly* 31 (June 1966): 153–78.

Index